Communities of Faith

A Way of Life

Introducing Hinduism

Ram Gidoomal and Robin Thomson

Hodder & Stoughton

LONDON SYDNEY AUCKLAND

Copyright © 1997 by Ram Gidoomal and Robin Thomson

First published in Great Britain in 1997

The right of Ram Gidoomal and Robin Thomson to be identified as
the Authors of the Work has been asserted by them in accordance
with the Copyright, Designs and Patents Act 1988.

1 3 5 7 9 10 8 6 4 2

British Library Cataloguing in Publication Data
A record for this book is available from the British Library

ISBN 0 340 66923 3

Typeset by Avon Dataset Ltd, Bidford-on-Avon, Warks

Printed and bound in Great Britain by
Clays Ltd. St Ives PLC, Bungay, Suffolk

Hodder and Stoughton
A division of Hodder Headline PLC
338 Euston Road
London NW1 3BH

Contents

Series Editor's Preface

There is a human tendency to try to present one's own beliefs, values and practices in a good light by deliberately presenting other beliefs, etc. in as bad a light as possible. In this series of books, the authors will not be guilty of misrepresentation, but will be guided by a basic Christian principle – that we should love our neighbours as we love ourselves. Therefore, the same respect and generosity will be given to each faith as Christians would wish for their own faith.

In this series on world faiths we are aiming to produce reference works which will be scholarly in terms of their accuracy and authority, completely fair to others, so that members of different faith communities will recognise themselves in the presentations, and also easily accessible to the general reader.

At the same time, they are written from a confident Christian perspective, and in each book the author will engage in a serious dialogue with the beliefs, values and practices of the faith which he/she is presenting. The authors all have genuine knowledge of the faith about which they are writing, personal experience of the community which holds that faith, a proven ability to reflect deeply on the issues involved, and the gift of being a good communicator. They are all practising Christians who are involved in dialogue with people of other faiths and cultures. Their interaction is sensitive and informed.

In each volume we shall explore a distinct faith and meet the community which lives by it. While the aim is to produce resources which capture the essential and timeless beliefs and values of each faith, full attention is given to the major contemporary issues and personalities. In the same way, while it is important to be aware of the global context of each faith, significant attention will be paid to the situation in the United Kingdom.

In order to make it easier to cross-reference among the books in this series, we have organised each book along the same lines. Topics dealt with in the numbered chapters will be the same in each book, no matter what the titles may be. You are therefore invited to join us in a great exploration of the world's faiths.

Hinduism is a world faith: its ideas are increasingly popular and widely accepted today. The devotion of Hindu people is striking, and their religious art can be inspiring. And yet it strikes many Westerners as compromised by its perceived fatalism. Can the rest of the world recognise the community of gods and goddesses which Hindus worship? Can Christians learn from a faith community which seems so different in every way? Ram Gidoomal and Robin Thomson lead us wisely through the Hindu world in this stimulating and satisfying book.

Walter Riggans

Acknowledgments

We are grateful to a number of people who helped us in writing this book. Paul Joshua and Andy Mason assisted with research and some initial drafts. Sarah Thomson prepared the glossary and index and Shoko Thomson typed the manuscript.

Our special thanks to Paul and Su East, Shakun Johnson, Sunil Kapur, Deepak and Celia Mahtani, Chandu Malkani, Chatru and Jyoti Manglani, C. V. Mathew, Steve and Meena Neumann, Sunil Rahcja, Arthur Rowe and Basil Scott, who read the manuscript at various stages and gave us helpful criticisms, suggestions and information.

I

Basic World-view

Asato ma sad gamaya
Tamaso ma jyotir gamaya
Mrutyor ma amrutam gamaya

From the unreal lead me to the real
From darkness lead me to light
From death lead me to immortality[1]

- The Ganga river at dawn. As the sun's rays touch the water, groups of men and women raise their hands in worship and immerse themselves in the river. On the bank, rows of *Brahmins**[2] sit in silent meditation under their umbrellas.
- A Bombay businesswoman stops her car on the way to the office. She stands in front of a small shrine, a roughly carved stone with an image of *Shiva**. Bowing her head, she prays and places an offering of fruit before the image. A priest puts red powder and sandalwood paste on her forehead.
- A nuclear scientist lectures on the new physics. 'All matter and consciousness are inter-connected. Behind everything that you see is pure energy, the only true reality. We Hindus call it *Brahman**.'
- Fifteen million people crowd together at the *Kumbh Mela* in Allahabad – the largest recorded number of human beings ever assembled together with a common purpose. In front of the enormous, heaving crowd are hundreds of naked *sadhus**, their hair matted and their bodies streaked

with ash, leading the way to the river bank.

- Another crowd, also led by *sadhus*, rushes towards the *Babri Masjid*, a Muslim building in Ayodhya. Waving their tridents, and hurling stones, they overpower the security guards and pull down the 400-year-old structure. Rioting spreads across India, leaving over one thousand dead and many more injured. Around the world temples and mosques are attacked in tit-for-tat retaliation.

- A philosopher sits cross-legged in calm detachment, talking quietly to his disciples about realisation. As they watch they are not sure whether he is still conscious or not, but his quiet words and the smile on his face have authority.

- Back in the 1960s, as 'Beatlemania' sweeps the world, the frenetic beat and rhythm of the guitars slide into the gentler notes of the *sitar*. The Beatles have been to Rishikesh and have 'realised' themselves through Maharishi Mahesh Yogi. The science of Transcendental Meditation spreads across the campuses and corporations of the USA and around the world.

- Outside temples in Delhi and Bombay, Bradford and Leicester, Hong Kong and Nairobi, long queues of people wait patiently to offer milk to their images and see them – miraculously – drinking. Offices lie empty. The telephones at the Bombay stock exchange remain unanswered. Milk supplies are completely sold out. 'God has a message for us,' says a priest. 'He is saying: this is not just a stone, but it is me.'

- A new factory is opening in Chicago. Before the chairman asks his wife to cut the ribbon, he beckons to a priest. The small crowd watches as he lights a fire, offers fruit and flowers and then leads the way round the building, chanting in Sanskrit and daubing red powder on each machine, computer and book of accounts.

- In the Albert Hall in London, a group kneel in front of their *guru**. Each devotee receives a secret *mantra** whispered in the ear and a picture of the guru to hang around their necks. They have started on their new journey of faith.

● An elderly couple sits in a large garden. Around them are
a group of middle-aged adults. Around them are a larger
group of young people – teenagers, boys in shorts, tod-
dlers and a baby in its mother's arms. A Hindu family
together. Shortly afterwards they will be joined by thirty
to forty other relatives for Sunday afternoon tea.

● On a makeshift election platform the speaker proclaims
the glories of ancient India and calls for the re-establishment of Hindutva and the rule of Ram. All will acknowledge the Hindu way, he declaims, especially minorities
who would be welcome back to the fold.

Symbols of Hinduism, the faith of over seven hundred million
people. But which is the real symbol? There seems to be a
bewildering variety, because in fact Hinduism does contain
so many different beliefs and practices. 'Hinduism, uniquely
among the major religions of the world, is a decentralised
system with no formal institutional controls.'[3]

Hinduism has a long history. Its followers call it 'the eternal
religion' (Sanatana Dharma*). Uniquely among the world's
religions, there is no single founder (chapters 2, 3). There are
volumes of scriptures (chapter 4) and six major schools of
philosophy. Hindus have widely different beliefs (chapters 3,
5) and follow widely different practices of spirituality and
worship (chapter 6).

The Hindu tradition is 'probably the most varied and
flexible religious system in the world'.[4] At the same time it is
based on the most stable social system (chapters 3, 8). Its
ethical requirements are elaborate from one perspective, very
simple from another (chapter 7). It is traditionally tolerant
but can also be militant (chapter 9).

This chapter is not a summary of Hinduism but tries to
look at it from different perspectives. The average Hindu (if
such a person exists) may see his or her faith from one or
more of these perspectives. Some will see it from all of them.
Eight key words in this chapter are in bold type. They express
major ideas, which we will look at further in the following
chapters.

A. The reality of God: the eternal search

'I don't know much about Hinduism; I just believe in God. I
follow what my mother taught me' (a devout Hindu lady).

For Hindus, God is naturally at the centre of life. If you
ask a Hindu which god she or he believes in, there may be
many answers. But behind all the different names is the
conviction that God is one. God is the ultimate and absolute
reality, the divine energy, the divine principle, the one behind
the many manifestations and phenomena of life which we
see and experience. This One is behind all things, at the centre
of all things, beyond all knowledge, known as *Brahman*.

> *Brahman* verily is this immortal being.
> In front is *Brahman*, behind is *Brahman*.
> To the right and to the left.
> It spreads forth above and below.
> Verily, *Brahman* alone is this glorious universe.[5]

For some, *Brahman*[6] is an impersonal principle, more like
energy. Many prayers begin or end with *OM**, the sacred
syllable which expresses the mystical fullness of God's Being.
It is considered to be the primal sound and vibration which
produces energy and includes past, present and future. It is
expressing what is actually inexpressible.

Others think of this ultimate reality as a personal God, with
whom the worshipper can have some kind of relationship.
They might refer to God as *Bhagwan** rather than *Brahman*.

If God is the ultimate reality, then the aim of life is to
find union with God. Many Hindus would agree with the
following:

Three central truths of the eternal law, the *Sanatana Dharma**,
are:

1. God exists.
2. People can come to know him.
3. The whole purpose of life is to come to know God.[7]

That may be more than the average person can hope for. They

may just have a vague desire for peace. They may just hope
to move at least one step forward in this life.

How? Why? There are many answers and many ways.
Philosophers seek for knowledge and realisation (*jnana**),
through meditation and the disciplines of *yoga**. Some seek
God through their devotion and love (*bhakti**). Others serve
God through selfless action (*karma**). These are the three
main paths to salvation in the classical tradition. Some follow
the way of sacrifice and ritual. Others seek the release of
energy (*shakti**) through esoteric practices.

Some say that God is already known in the Self within us
(*atman**). *Vedanta** is the school of thought most associated
with this view and the best known school of Hinduism in the
West.

But this view is not universal and many Hindus would
struggle with the idea of God as identical with themselves.
For them their God is personal, one whom they seek and
whose grace they need (chapters 5,6,10). Jitu Patel is the co-
owner of Europa Foods, one of the fastest growing super-
market chains in London. He is also a committed member of
the Swaminarayan Mission, with its gleaming new temple in
Neasden. He draws strength for his demanding business from
his faith in God: 'This faith gives you immense energy and
courage from within to go ahead. Everything just falls into
place. It's as if the Lord is there getting me through this maze
and gives me the right energy and the right time and the right
opportunity. I have immense faith in the Lord.'[8]

B. The problems of life: wrestling with issues

Life is a struggle. It is full of pain, suffering, injustice. The
world is manifestly an unfair place. Why? Men and women
in every time and place and culture have wrestled with these
questions. They led Prince Gautama to leave the luxuries of
the palace to find answers in the forest and become the
Buddha. Hindu philosophers have come up with the most
logical and rigorous analysis of the problems of life. 'India in
particular furnishes ... examples of every conceivable type
of attempt at the solution of the religious problem.'[9]

The answer is seen in the law of *karma*. This is the most

strict law of cause and effect in the moral realm. 'Whatever a man sows that will he also reap.' Whatever you do, good or bad, you will reap the consequences, good or bad.

This is logical and it works for much of life, both the physical and moral realms. But what about the person who is obviously corrupt, but dies rich, apparently quite at ease? And what about the person who starts life with a handicap – poverty, disease, an orphan? The law of cause and effect does not appear to be working out. The philosophers who wrestled with this question concluded that it was not enough to apply it in this life. The principle must be extended to a whole succession of lives, past and future. Within this series of rebirths there is ample opportunity for the law of cause and effect to work itself out.

At some point belief in reincarnation became firmly fixed, probably about 1000 BC. It is known as *sansara**, the wheel or cycle of birth, death and rebirth.

There is no escape from *karma*. 'It is automatic and inerrant. Just as a calf would find out its mother out of a thousand other cows, so *karma* will always find the person to whom it belongs.'[10] The only hope is to improve your situation in successive lives, so that eventually you can escape from the cycle. This is called *moksha**, release or liberation.

You can go backward or forward in the cycle. Somebody who lives badly will go backward, being reborn as a human being at a lower level of life or fortune, or as an animal of higher or lower degree, and so on down the scale. Someone who lives well moves upward, to the final possibility of *moksha*.

Karma and *sansara*, the cycle of birth and re-birth, have become the twin pillars of Hindu belief, its most basic presupposition. If there is anything which all Hindus – or almost all – believe without question, it is this.

C. The daily round: doing your duty

Karma is a basic presupposition of life, beneath the surface all the time. For some, especially those better off in life, it is a powerful motive for seeking good or avoiding evil. It's quite comforting to know that your *karma* must have been good, because your present situation is not unpleasant.

But thinking about rebirth and *karma* may be quite abstract. Even thinking about God may be distant for some, far removed from daily life. How do I live from day to day? Another central feature of Hinduism is the idea of *dharma**.

Dharma can be translated 'religion'. In that sense it is used to describe the whole range of Hindu belief and practice. It is a principle that sustains the universe, like *karma*. 'I believe in *dharma*, the ultimate power. *Dharma* gives me strength,'[11] says Sanjay Dutt, one of India's best known film stars, the equivalent of Sylvester Stallone. At present he is facing trial on charges connected with the major bomb blasts in Bombay in 1993.

That is the broad, over-arching meaning of the word. At the level of the individual, it describes the 'duty' or responsibility that each of us must fulfil. This is not defined in a list of absolute commands like the Ten Commandments. It is rather expressed in relationships. Your duty depends on who you are. Your duty is to fulfil your role in your particular situation (chapter 7). You have your duty to the gods, to your guru, and according to your place in the social structure (chapters 3, 8). The great stories and epics of the Hindu tradition are about people who fulfilled their *dharma* in this way. Recently, a father with five daughters fulfilled his *dharma* by providing adequate dowries for each of them. In response his three sons fulfilled their *dharma* by taking care of their own needs.

Doing your duty, fulfilling your *dharma*, could be the best summary of the Hindu way of life. It also leads us to the next perspective on Hinduism.

D. The social structure: fitting into your place

Dharma is always fulfilled in relationship, because all of life is a network of relationships. From one perspective Hinduism is the most individualistic religion in the world. Each individual is subject to his own unique law of *karma*, his unique destiny, which cannot be transferred. But no individual in Hinduism is ever alone. Every Hindu is born into a family, the most basic unit of the social structure. Being part of your family is the essence of Hinduism. Mahēndra Singhal, a professor of mathematics in Chicago, remembers his childhood:

> I was raised in a rigidly-structured and despotically-ruled Hindu home with well-preserved traditions, well-devoted customs, and well-formulated expectations, along with, of course, a great deal of love, understanding, and exhortation. You imbibed the family culture, as it were, by being a member of the family, and you emulated the family's perspective on history, art, and religion, by repeated reminders, to enhance the family's image in the local community. Into such a wonderfully strict and kind family I was born.

The Hindu family is not just father and mother with 2.4 children. It is parents and grandparents, living together under the same roof. So that means cousins, aunts and uncles, all part of the immediate family. Then there are other cousins, aunts and uncles on your mother's side, not to mention second cousins, in-laws, great aunts and uncles . . .

This extended family is part of the larger social unit known as the *caste*. Caste is the most important structure of Hinduism, which has held it all together for thousands of years (chapters 3, 8).

Each person must fulfil their role within this structure, including their duty to other members of the family and caste, for example as a father, mother, brother protecting his sisters and so on. The roles are clearly marked out, for men and women. For a man there are four *stages*, and four legitimate *goals* in life (see chapters 3, 7, 8).

A very important feature of family life is the performance of rituals (chapter 6). These maintain family life, the worship of the gods and the structures of existence. There is daily worship (individual and corporate), including prayer and meditation, attending to the images, or times of fasting. There are festivals to mark the seasons of the year or special events of the past. There are rituals to mark the stages of life, from birth, the child's naming day, the first hair cutting, the sacred thread ceremony, marriage, childbirth, and on finally to death.

Astrology and the phases of the moon are crucial in regulating the events of life. The religious calendar follows the lunar year.

When a young couple want to get married, the first thing their parents do is to check their horoscopes. From these the priest can advise whether they match each other, and if so, the most auspicious time for the wedding (usually in the early hours of the morning). Astrology is based on the power of the heavenly bodies. They determine the pattern of life on earth and every human being is caught up in that intricate design. Hindu astrology is highly developed and no event in life can pass without consulting the astrologers. Birthdays, weddings, funerals, inaugurating a business, the timing of the elections, choosing cabinet ministers – all depend on their guidance. These days many of them are computerised, which speeds things up!

Women have a key place in maintaining this structure of existence through the regular round of rituals. A woman's role is not independent. Her goal is to please her father first and then her brothers, who are responsible to protect her. When she marries she passes to the care of her husband. From now on her goal in life is to please him and then to bring up her children (under the watchful eye of her mother-in-law).

Women maintain the social structure of Hinduism, which in turn maintains Hinduism. The other key group is the priests, traditionally Brahmins, who have controlled Hinduism through the centuries.

Through performing duties and rituals, you are maintaining solidarity with the rest of the family and the caste. As long as you stay in this structure, you are accepted as a part of Hinduism (whatever you may believe or not believe).

E. The gods: honouring divine powers

While God is One and is thought of by some in abstract terms, the gods are many and are seen as personal. God is the One Reality, but manifested in many different aspects, depending on the situation and needs of each individual. That is why there are so many gods and goddesses – usually reckoned at three hundred and thirty million. This figure is

based on a reference in the *Vedas** (the oldest Hindu scriptures), though some scholars say that it should really be
translated 'thirty-three'.

The gods may be seen as forces of nature, the sun, the
moon, wind, rain, light, fire, desire. They are guardians of
morality, upholding the laws of *karma* and fate. They can
punish those who transgress them. They are objects of devotion. Through their images, worshippers give honour and
recognition to the gods. They attend them and serve them as
kings and queens with royal power, both in daily worship
and at special festivals. They bring their petitions and requests
to them.

OM jay jagdish hare, swami jay jagdish hare
Hail to thee, lord of the universe, remover of sorrow and
    Master of all
Shraddha bhakti badhao, santan ki seva
Bless me with ever-increasing faith, divine love and spirit of
    service[12]

With so many gods and goddesses, the pantheon can be very
elaborate (chapter 5). But some can explain it quite clearly,
like Dr Mehta in Delhi: 'The family of the gods is basically
simple. At the top is Mataji*, the Mother Goddess. Then
there are three others – Brahma*, Vishnu*, Shiva. They have
their consorts, Saraswati, Lakshmi and Parvati, who represent their *shakti* [power]. All the other gods are either aspects
of one of these three, or their lieutenants.'

The lives of the gods and their powers and exploits are
celebrated in vast collections of myths and stories. These tell
about the relationships of the gods with each other and with
human beings. They explain the power structure of the universe and how one ought to behave within it. Some of the
gods have come down into the world at different times, taking
human or animal form, in order to uphold righteousness.
These are known as *avatars** (chapter 5).

Hinduism has many stories. Unlike Christianity, for example, there is no 'main' story about God's intervention in
history. That would be seen as a limitation. 'Every Hindu

myth is different; all Hindu myths are alike. In spite of the
deep-seated, totally compelling world-view that moulds every
image and symbol, every word and idea . . . each myth celebrates the belief that the universe is boundlessly various, that
everything occurs simultaneously, that all possibilities may
exist without excluding each other.'[13]

Does this diversity suggest the idea that all ways lead to
God?

Some celebrate this luxuriant diversity and the range of
options which it brings. Others find it bewildering. And so
they turn with relief to those who can teach them with clarity
and authority. The gurus are key figures of Hinduism. Their
role is to clear a path through the jungle, a straight path
which can lead to God and the fulfilment of life. We shall
return to the gurus in every chapter of this book.

F. The world of nature: linked or detached?

Nature is very important for Hindus. All of life is inter-
connected. There is a strong emphasis on the fertility of the
land and people. At the centre of the popular idea of the
universe is Mount Meru. The gods live on Mount Kailash.
Rivers, trees, snakes, animals and plants are all throbbing
with life. For the sophisticated, this represents the divine
energy of the universe; the majority of Hindus, especially in
the villages, are conscious of spirits behind them, needing to
be placated through offerings or rituals. Cows are specially
venerated as symbols of provision and plenty. They wander
freely in the streets of any Indian town or city.

At the same time there is a feeling of detachment, a sense
that nature is ultimately unreal, or at least belongs to a second
order of reality. For some this attitude is based on the idea
that nature is *maya**. This word is often translated 'illusion'
and for some it does mean just that. The average Hindu
would not go so far. There are other ways to translate this
word, such as 'creative power'.

We find the same ambivalent attitude towards the body.
More than any other religion, Hinduism celebrates the body
and bodily pleasures. The *Kama Sutra* is one Hindu text
which thousands have heard of (though very few actually

know its contents). The erotic sculptures of the Khajuraho temples in North India attract thousands of tourists. But Hinduism is also the home of the philosophy and practice of *yoga*, whose aim is total control and rigid mastery of the body. The exercises of *yoga* are designed to control the entrances and exits to the body, to maintain clinical purity in it, to master its breathing and ultimately to shut it down altogether, so that the soul can be free from its confines and escape from the body.

Hinduism is the home of the most spectacular forms of asceticism. The holy man lying on his bed of nails, the wandering beggar with only his loin cloth and begging bowl, the *sannyasi** who has given up all to meditate in the forest, are its symbols.

Where does it all lead?
Hindus give different answers:

>'Realisation is the goal,' say those who follow the way of knowledge *(jnana marg)*.
>
>'Give yourself to God in devotion. Depend on his grace,' say those who follow the path of devotion (*bhakti marg*).
>
>'Do your duty and fulfil your place in society,' say those who believe in the way of action and service *(karma marg*)*.
>
>'The search for peace,' is the answer that many give. *Shanti** (peace) is one of the most evocative words in Hinduism. *Om, Shanti, Shanti* are the closing words of many prayers.

Ed Viswanathan, a Hindu in the USA, answers questions from his fourteen-year-old son:

>'Daddy, what do you or anyone try to achieve through the practice of Hinduism?'
>
>'It is easy to say "salvation", but that is the ultimate goal. Right now, we are trying to achieve peace and harmony in life . . . The Hindu way of life aids that effort . . . As I told you before, it is quite easy to follow Hinduism, because Hinduism believes that ignorance is the root of all

evil and true knowledge is the answer to all problems. First, try to understand the truth, and then try to practise and realise that truth.

'So, most of us who adhere to Hinduism are not trying to become gurus or hermits or philosophers. We are just trying to have a stress-free, peaceful life.'[14]

At the very least, you can hope that the next life will be better than this one.

Conclusion

Hinduism is the most diverse of all the great religions of the world. It has a remarkable tolerance, openness to ideas from all directions and acceptance of life, in the face of all its contradictions and struggles.

Contrary to a popular misconception often encountered in the West, Hinduism is not a passive, world-negating religion. It is verily a vibrant, life-affirming faith, using 'life' in the deeper sense of that supreme poise that transcends the dualities of life and death. According to the Hindu view, there is a supreme state into which it is possible for the human consciousness to enter and which, once achieved, places one above the endless cycle of rebirth in which the entire cosmos is imprisoned.[15]

Hinduism has a great concern for truth. '*Satyam Eva Jayate*' – 'Truth alone will triumph' – are the closing words of the film *Gandhi* and the motto of the Indian Republic.[16] Hinduism has wrestled with the problems of life and produced its answers to the questions of existence. It seeks to bring a harmony and synthesis of all religions. It is based on a rigid, unbending social structure and yet it fosters the most radical individualism. It has given birth to three other major religions – Buddhism, Jainism and Sikhism. It has spread across South East Asia in previous centuries. And in the last thirty years it has provided the foundations of the New Age Movement.

Reflection

Hinduism is truly a world religion. It provides the major alternative to the Judaeo-Christian world-view and the closely related Islamic world-view. In the following chapters we explore different facets of Hindu belief and experience. We shall reflect further on how they relate to other religions and world-views in chapters 9 and 10.

1. An ancient Sanskrit prayer from the *Rig Veda*, the earliest Hindu scriptures.
2. Sanskrit words are usually printed in italics. An asterisk * on the first use of a word indicates a word listed in the glossary (pages 168–71).
3. Michael Nagler, quoted in Eknath Easwaran, *The Upanishads* (Penguin, London, 1987), p. 251.
4. T. J. Hopkins, *The Hindu Religious Tradition: The Religious Life of Man* (Wadsworth Publishing Company, Belmont, CA, 1971), p. 86.
5. *Mundakya Upanishad* 2.2.12.
6. Three words are closely related but have different meanings:
    Brahman: the Absolute God.
    Brahmin: one of the major castes, traditionally the priests. This word can also be spelt Brahman, but is usually spelt Brahmin to avoid confusion.
    Brahma: one of the separate deities, usually associated with Vishnu and Shiva (chapter 5).
7. Ram Gidoomal and Mike Fearon, *Karma 'n' Chips* (Wimbledon Publishing Co, London, 1994), p. 31.
8. *Evening Standard*, 12 August 1996.
9. A. C. Bouquet, *Comparative Religion*, quoted by K. M. Sen, *Hinduism* (Pelican Books, London, 1961), p. 11.
10. Acharya Daya Prakash, *The Fulfilment of the Vedic Quest* (Lucknow Publishing House, Lucknow, 1982), p. 20. He is quoting from the *Mahabharata**, one of the great epics of Hinduism.
11. *Telegraph Magazine*, 26 October 1996.
12. The first and last lines of a prayer sung daily in many temples.
13. Wendy Doniger O' Flaherty, in Betty Radice, *Hindu Myths* (Penguin, London, 1975), p. 11.

14. Ed Viswanathan, *Am I a Hindu? The Hinduism Primer* (Rupa and Co, Calcutta, 1993), p. 312.
15. Karan Singh, *Essays on Hinduism* (Ratna Sagar, Delhi, 1990), p. 4.
16. The words come from the *Mundaka Upanishad* 3.1.6.

2

Key Figures in Hinduism

May that elephant-faced God [Ganesha] whom Shiva worshipped before conquering Tripura; Vishnu worshipped before tying up Maha Bali; Brahma worshipped before starting creation; Sesh Nag worshipped before carrying the earth on its heads; Parvati worshipped before destroying Mahishasura; the Siddhas worshipped for accomplishments and the god of love worshipped before conquering the universe – may he protect us.[1]

Hinduism has no founder. There is no figure like Buddha, Jesus, Confucius or Mohammed. Many people played strategic roles in its evolution, but the Hindu tradition does not emphasise any individual or group of leaders. Many of the key figures are unknown. 'One of the characteristics of ancient Hindu thought is its indifference to history . . . ancient Indian writers care more for the truth of experience . . . than for the circumstances that gave it birth.'[2]

It is not just that dates and personalities are unimportant. There are many perspectives. One Hindu's list of significant leaders may not be accepted by another. So picking key figures and giving a historical survey is not as straightforward as you might expect. In this chapter we look at five characters representing five key areas:

- law and social structure
- theology
- devotional piety
- social reform

- political liberation.

Then we look at two significant trends in the last fifty years.

1. The earliest period: Manu the lawgiver

Manu* represents the beginning. A semi-divine, mythical figure, he is the first man, the first king of India, the first to light the sacrificial fire, the first and greatest lawgiver. Romila Thapar sums up the mythological tradition:

> The first king of India was Manu Svayambhu (self-born Manu). Manu was born directly of the god Brahma, and was a hermaphrodite. From the female half of his body he bore two sons and three daughters, from whom descended a series of Manus. But the tenth Manu was the most famous of them all. It was when he ruled over the earth that the great flood occurred, when everything was submerged and only Manu survived. The human race began from Manu and his family.[3]

Manu represents Hinduism in its early and classical period – roughly the first two thousand years. The traditions about Manu as the first man and king go right back to the beginnings. The *Laws of Manu,* a collection ascribed to the mythical lawgiver, were written down only about 200 BC, toward the end of the classical period.[4] They represent the highly organised social structure which had been developed by that time and which has carried Hinduism forward since then. In between, profound changes had taken place.

Beginnings

The early history of Hinduism is linked with the earliest history of India and its civilisation. Not much was known about the original people of the land until early this century, when archaeologists excavated two cities in the Indus River valley, in what is now Pakistan. The remains of Mohenjodaro and Harappa revealed a highly developed society, known as the Indus Valley Civilisation, dating back to about 2500 BC. (British railway engineers had discovered some of the ruins

in the nineteenth century but were more interested in using
the rubble for their railway. Today the railway line between
Multan and Lahore runs on the secure foundation of bricks
over 4000 years old.)[5]

We cannot read the language on the few inscriptions left
by the Indus Valley Civilisation and so our knowledge of it is
incomplete. We get a glimpse of its religion from some of the
remains. They worshipped various gods and goddesses, including perhaps a mother goddess and possibly a forerunner
of the great Hindu God Shiva. They seem to have greatly
valued ritual purity, judging by elaborate bathing facilities in
each house and also in a public place. There were apparently
no temples.

We do not know what connections the Indus Valley Civilisation had with people living in other parts of India, usually
believed to be the Dravidians. We do not know, either, how
it came to an end – perhaps through flooding around 1700
BC, perhaps through invasion. All we know is that by about
1500 BC the plains of North West India were occupied by
people who referred to themselves as Aryans. They composed
hymns which were collected together between 1500 and 1000
BC. They are known as the *Rig Veda**, the earliest part of the
massive collection of the *Vedas* (chapter 4).

The Aryans emigrated from somewhere north of Iran. They
were related to similar peoples who moved to Western
Europe, Iran and other parts of the Middle East. Their
language, Sanskrit, came from an Indo-European ancestor,
and so is related to Latin and Greek. Their religious beliefs
and practices were similar to those of other peoples of the
Middle East (such as Mesopotamia and Canaan) and also to
the religions of Greece and Rome (chapters 4, 5).

From the Creator God to the gods

There are signs of early belief in one Creator God, but the
hymns of the *Rig Veda* reflect a pantheon of many gods,
representing forces of nature, similar to the Indo-European
gods. During this period there must have been a gradual
fusion of the cultures and beliefs of the Aryans and the
indigenous peoples, but it is hard to trace details.

From the gods to the sacrifice

Sacrifice played an important part in their lives. The early sacrifices were joyful offerings to the gods. As time went on the sacrifices were seen not just as an offering to the gods but as the way of unifying and maintaining the whole of existence, including the gods. So they became the means of ordering, understanding and ultimately controlling the universe. For this it was necessary to perform the sacrifices in the right way. And for this it was of course necessary to have priests who knew how to do things in the right way. So the priests became more and more important, controlling religion and the whole of life through ritual and sacrifice.

The later *Vedas* (chapter 4) reflect this transition from hymns to ritual instructions to magic formulae. The priests ruled.

The sixth-century revolt

The sixth century BC saw a revolt against the power of the priests. It was not only in India. A tidal wave seems to have swept across the ancient world, from Zoroaster in Persia, to Buddha and Mahavir in India, to Confucius and Lao-Tse in China. They all represent a move away from dead ritual to something more inward – ethical behaviour, or withdrawal from desire, or conformity to the Way. One group in India, the Charvakas, were atheists. They denied the existence of any god and said that happiness was the highest goal.

Buddha and Mahavir became the founders of new religions, Buddhism (with all its later developments) and Jainism. Buddhist teaching spread rapidly among those who were frustrated with the priestly religion, especially when the Emperor Ashoka, who controlled almost the whole of India, publicly embraced Buddhism (about 260 BC). Jainism emphasised right conduct, especially *ahimsa** or non-violence. It was through Jainism that vegetarianism spread through India (chapter 7).

From the sacrifice to the One: the journey inwards

These major challenges to the system came in the sixth century but they had already been preceded by an inward movement within Hinduism. The *Upanishads** (chapter 4) are a series of philosophical poems and meditations, written around 900–700 BC. They moved behind the gods of nature and the ritual of the sacrifices to the One Reality and Principle beneath them all, Brahman.

The *Upanishads* were the foundation of Hindu thought and philosophy and introduced some of its most distinctive beliefs. They provided a way of thinking about God and reality called monism, which has retained its influence through the centuries and is being powerfully rediscovered today, especially in the New Age Movement (chapters 4, 5). They offered a way to the knowledge of God without ritual, a deeper meaning behind the sacrifices. They said that the inner Self was as much a reflection of absolute reality as the absolute Brahman. The goal of life was union with the One, through realising this unity (chapter 5). So meditation played an important part in the spiritual life. The *Upanishads* also introduced the concepts of *karma* and reincarnation, which became fundamental beliefs of Hinduism.

Popular religion

The *Upanishads* provided an inner emphasis as deep and radical as the teaching of Buddha. But the religion they represented was severely individualistic. It could only be for the few. In the centuries after the rise of Buddhism, we find the reappearance of more popular and accessible features of Hinduism. People turned back to the worship of the gods. Popular stories of the gods circulated in abundance and were written down as Epics and later the *Puranas**, 'Stories of Ancient Times' (chapter 4). The worship of the gods was helped through the increasing use of images and the development of temples, something comparatively new in the Hindu tradition. The discipline of meditation was established and the basic text on *yoga* by Patanjali was written (around the first century AD). Above all, the priests emphasised the practice of duty in religion. They established the social structure of Hinduism, as summed up in the famous *Laws of Manu*.

An ordered life

The *Laws of Manu* (written down about 200 BC) laid down the way in which each person should live and fulfil their duty or *dharma*. Manu affirmed the four major castes into which all human beings are divided (except for those outside the system). He laid down four goals of life and four stages of life for a Hindu man. And he prescribed the role of a Hindu woman in relation to her father, brothers and husband.

The *Laws of Manu* were considered to be 'medicine'. Here he prescribes the procedure for naming a male child:

> The name-giving should be done on the tenth day after birth or the twelfth day, or on an excellent lunar day, or moment, or under a constellation that has good qualities. The name of a priest should have a word for auspiciousness, of a ruler strength, of a commoner property, and the name of a servant should breed disgust. The name of a priest should have a word for secure comfort, of a king it should have protection, of a commoner it should be connected with prosperity, of a servant it should be connected with service. The names of women should be easy to pronounce, not harsh, of patent meaning, and auspicious; they should captivate the mind-and-heart, end in a long vowel, and contain a word for blessings.[6]

The *Bhagavad Gita** also expressed this classical synthesis of philosophy, belief, practice and social stability. We shall examine it more closely in chapter 4.

All of life was now ordered in a stable social structure. There was room for diversity of thought and even practice, but the priests remained firmly in control.

2. The re-establishment of theology: Sankara the theologian

Popular religion continued to thrive in the centuries after Manu and the *Bhagavad Gita*. Images and temples continued to multiply. The old Vedic sacrifices were replaced by a new form of worship – *puja** – which became standard from now on (chapter 6).

The amazing cave temples of Ellora were developed in this period. Their bold sculptures of the gods show the brilliance and vitality of the art of this time. The climax was the giant Kailasa temple, carved out of a single solid rock, two and a half times the size of the Parthenon, 100 feet high. It took over a hundred years to build. The last architect expressed his feelings in an inscription: 'Wonderful! O how could I ever have done it?' Further south, the exquisite shore temples at Mahabalipuram were another masterpiece.

Popular Hinduism had weathered the challenges of Buddhism and Jainism. It had spread out beyond the esoteric teaching of the *Upanishads*. But there were wide varieties of teaching and practice. The stories of the *Puranas* (chapter 4) were entertaining, but some considered them fanciful. Not all the religious revival stayed within the orthodox boundaries set by the *Vedas* and priests. Some groups developed new rituals. Others expressed passionate devotion to their gods, especially Vishnu and Shiva. A South Indian group was called the *Alvars**, which meant literally 'the divers into God'. Others emphasised the cult of the Mother Goddess or the feminine principle. They developed rituals and practices known as *tantra**.

Hinduism was moving in several directions at once. Could it maintain a unified tradition, or would the streams continue to flow separately?

This was how it appeared to a young man who lived only thirty-two years but was a philosophical and theological giant. He re-established Hindu thought, firmly excluded unorthodox views like Buddhism and Jainism, and established *Advaita Vedanta** as the major philosophical school within Hinduism.

Sankara (788–820 AD) was born to a South Indian Brahmin couple who had been childless for a long time, in answer to prayers directed to Lord Shiva. He mastered the *Vedas* while still young and at six or seven resolved to become a *sannyasi* or ascetic (chapter 8). His mother was unwilling but while Sankara was bathing in a river, he was caught by a crocodile. He called out for permission to become a *sannyasi*. His mother thought he was going to die, so she agreed. Immediately the crocodile let him go.

Sankara went to North India and found a guru on the banks of the river Narmada. Govindapada, his teacher, found him exceptionally gifted and sent him on to Varanasi, the spiritual centre of Hinduism. Here he got to grips with his philosophy, resulting in his commentaries on the *Upanishads*. His most famous work was the *Brahma Sutra Bhashya*: a commentary on the *Brahma Sutras*.

As his popularity grew Sankara attracted many disciples. He decided to travel to the four corners of India to propagate his philosophy and to establish four monasteries, which are still flourishing today. Sankara loved debating with his opponents from other philosophical schools, and especially with Buddhists and Jains. He converted many back to Hinduism.

Sankara was revered as an embodiment of Lord Shiva himself. His philosophy was called *advaita**, that is monism or non-duality, based on the *Upanishads* (chapters 4, 5). It was a response to two basic observations:

1. The scriptures and some people's experience taught that there is only one ultimate reality.
2. In daily life reality appears to be divided and changing, filled with individuals.

Sankara taught that these two observations were compatible. Brahman, the ultimate reality, is beyond change and even description. The *atman*, or essential Self within a person, is identical with Brahman. But we are bound by our ego and the physical world of change and plurality, until we realise that this is caused by *maya*, superimposing false impressions on what is real. Sankara's famous illustration was the man who sees a snake on the path. He is terrified, until he realises that it is only a rope. We are caught up in *maya*, until we realise our true nature.

Sankara's solution was radical and brilliantly simple. But it was hard for most people to square with their experience. Is there really no distinction between the self and God? Is the world around us completely unreal? What about a personal God?

So others tried to modify his system, especially two other South Indian philosophers, Ramanuja* (about 1100 AD) and Madhava* (about 1200 AD). We shall return to their views in chapter 5.

3. Devotional piety: Chaitanya the devotee

The way of devotion or *bhakti* has always been a part of Hindu tradition. The *Bhagavad Gita* recognised it as one of the three major ways to God. For some this longing for God spilled over into intense, extravagant expressions of love and devotion. Beginning from the Alvars in the sixth century, we can trace a whole succession of groups over the following centuries. They expressed their relationship with God in terms of human emotions – love, friendship, joy, suffering. Some focused on a particular god – Vishnu or Shiva. Others focused on an incarnation of God – most frequently Rama* or Krishna*, incarnations of Vishnu. They emphasised God's grace to the worshipper:

There is not a despicable deed which I have not committed
  a thousand times.
I am helplessly weeping . . . before thee, O redeemer
  of men!
O Infinite Being! Drowning as I am in the expansive sea of
  Sansara,
I seem to have reached a shore on resorting to thy feet.
A drop from the nectar ocean of love to the lovely
  lotus feet
extinguishes in an instant the blazing forest fire of
  transmigratory existence
and bestows supreme bliss.[7]

The *bhakti* movement cut across social boundaries. Men and women, kings and beggars, Brahmins and low caste all shared alike in these movements. They wanted to show that God was accessible:

God is my ancestor, the creator is my kinsman,
The world-guru is my caste, I am a child of the Almighty[8]

Amidst the pressures and changes caused by the Muslim invasions of this period, some *bhakti* movements included Muslims as well, such as Kabir the weaver. He was followed by Nanak, who tried to combine elements of Hinduism and Islam and ended up starting a new religion – Sikhism. Movements sprang up across India, from the Tamil country in the south to Kashmir in the north, from Maharashtra in the west to Bengal in the east. They were led by a succession of poet-saints, such as Namdev, Eknath, Tukaram, Kabir, Tulsidas, Vidyapati, Mirabai. They sang of their devotion in the vernacular languages, not Sanskrit, the language of religious texts. So 'religion was brought home to the hearts of the common people through songs which they could all understand'.

Chaitanya (1485–1533 AD) is of interest because of his inspiration to the International Society For Krishna Consciousness (ISKCON), better known as the Hare Krishna movement of today.

Chaitanya was very mischievous as a boy and the only way to stop him was the repeated mention of God's name. Two events changed his life: his brother's decision to renounce the world, and his father's death. At his father's funeral he met a *sannyasi* who convinced him of the virtues of devotion to Krishna. Chaitanya joined a group of Krishna devotees. Soon he decided to renounce the world and become a *sannyasi,* following Lord Krishna full-time.

Chaitanya reorganised the structure and method of devotion to Krishna. He introduced a public *kirtan** or worship through singing. He would walk the streets with his fellow devotees, singing and chanting the praises of Lord Krishna, with music and dancing. These processions were very emotional, with trembling and weeping, reaching almost hysterical proportions. They went on for long periods, well into the night. The idea was to create the atmosphere that existed in Vrindaban, the place where Krishna's devotees met him and enjoyed him intimately.

Large numbers were drawn to this new teaching and devotion. Chaitanya's message was simple. The most important pursuit in life is love for Lord Krishna. Ecstatic singing and dancing are the way to encounter him. Constant imagination of the love between Krishna and Radha (his favourite lover) is the way to free oneself of all thoughts of this life and its cares. The intimacy they enjoyed is the state that all Krishna devotees ought to strive for.

4. Renaissance: Ram Mohun Roy the social reformer

The end of the eighteenth century found India's civilisation and culture at a very low ebb. 'In that dark period nothing of first rate importance was produced in any language. There were no new developments in Hinduism and almost all indigenous arts languished and died for lack of patronage and appreciation.'[9]

The impact of the Muslim invasions had been absorbed in the previous centuries. Now came the very different invasion of Western military and economic power, accompanied by the silent influence of education, science, literature, history and religious beliefs. For about 150 years, between 1750 and 1900, Hinduism went through a period that has come to be known as its Renaissance.

One of the earliest renaissance figures was **Raja Ram Mohun Roy** (1772–1833). He was born into an orthodox Brahmin family and educated both in the traditional Hindu manner and also in Arabic and Persian literature and philosophy. At sixteen, he wrote a paper questioning idolatry in Hinduism. At forty-three, he retired in Calcutta, where he pursued religious and social reform, based on the dignity of all life and the futility of superstition. He was also convinced of the ethical superiority of monotheistic religion.

Roy targeted practices like sati*, the custom in which Hindu widows died on their husbands' funeral pyre. He opposed idolatry and the severe penalties for those who broke dietary laws, while thieves or murderers could get away by performing ceremonies and donating gifts to priests.

In 1828 Roy formed the *Brahmo Samaj* or Theistic Society, with the aim of promoting a lofty theism and restoring the religious purity of Hinduism, in keeping with Vedantic teaching. He translated the Vedanta into Bengali. Here he attempted to convey his idea of the unity of Brahman as the eternal and everlasting one, the personal creator and sustainer of the universe, worthy of all worship.

Ram Mohun Roy was a prolific writer and editor in English, Persian and Bengali. He supported the translation of English scientific and literary texts into Bengali and pro- vided for the publication of a Bengali grammar.

Roy aimed to make Hinduism rationally and ethically acceptable. He was followed by a brilliant succession of leaders committed to intellectual, spiritual and social reform. The *Brahmo Samaj* in Bengal was led by Debendranath Tagore, K. C. Sen and others. It was very open to science and to Western and Christian values. A quite different movement, called the *Arya Samaj*, was founded in the Punjab by Swami Dayananda (1824–83). 'Back to the Vedas!' was his slogan. The Vedas, he said, taught monotheism and morality, not idolatry, caste distinction, superstitions and evil social practices. The *Arya Samaj* was active in preaching social reform and bringing people back to Hinduism from Islam or Christianity. The poet Rabindranath Tagore won the Nobel Prize for Literature in 1913 and founded Shantiniketan Uni- versity near Calcutta.

Two key figures of the nineteenth century were **Ramakrishna** and **Swami Vivekananda**. Ramakrishna was a priest of the Kali temple, who experienced virtually every aspect of the Hindu tradition – meditation, visions, ecstasy, *bhakti*, *tantra* and identity with Brahman. He worshipped Kali, Vishnu and Shiva and also saw visions of Mohammed and Jesus. For him all religions were branches of the same tree.

Ramakrishna's favourite disciple was Narendranath, later known as Swami Vivekananda. Vivekananda travelled all over India with a small band of fellow disciples. He realised India's essential unity, along with its extremes of wealth and poverty. At its southernmost point, Kanayakumari, he had a vision of the motherland and what he must do to restore her former glory. He committed himself to the service of India, particularly the poor, through education, service, social reform and re-awakening of spiritual life.

Vivekananda became a powerful force to bring Hinduism to the world, especially through the Parliament of World Religions in Chicago in 1893 (chapter 3). And he brought into Hinduism powerful new elements of social concern and service.

5. Socio-political struggle: Gandhi the political liberator

The most important Hindu figure of the twentieth century was **Mahatma Gandhi** (1869–1948), the father of the nation. Gandhi's life and his political and social achievements are well known. We focus here on the way this sprang out of his understanding of Hinduism. Gandhi developed a completely new synthesis in which the spiritual, social and political were fused together. He openly acknowledged the influence of other faiths, especially Christian teaching and practice, and incorporated them into his own philosophy. But he remained essentially a Hindu and died with the name of Ram on his lips.

Mohandas Karamchand Gandhi was born in Porbandar in what is now Gujerat. The influence of his home and Hindu upbringing guided him throughout his life. When he was about thirteen he married Kasturba. At nineteen he went to England to study law.

His two extended periods in South Africa were very significant. Here his basic religious, economic, social and political philosophies took shape. One of the turning points was his experience of being thrown out of a train, because of his race. Gandhi's strategy to fight the racist laws was unique, based on the principle of *satyagraha**, fighting for truth through passive resistance. The more Gandhi worked with the poor, the more he realised their simplicity and its attractiveness. Influenced by Tolstoy and Ruskin, he gradually altered his lifestyle to reflect self-sufficiency and humility.

Gandhi developed a unique blend of values from Hindu and other sources. For him the two 'immortal maxims' of the Hindu scriptures were *ahimsa* (non-violence) and *satya** (truth). He regarded truth as the highest principle – in fact truth was God. He called his autobiography *My Experiments With Truth*. As he read the *Bhagavad Gita*, the Sermon on the Mount and Tolstoy's book *The Kingdom of God is Within You,* he formulated his doctrine of *ahimsa* as 'passive resistance to evil, wherever it is found'. He also called this *satyagraha,* 'truth force', or in other words resisting evil through voluntary suffering. He led campaigns of civil disobedience in South Africa and later in India, against racial discrimination, imperial rule in India, untouchability and Hindu–Muslim divisions. The impact was profound, both on those who participated and on those against whom the campaigns were directed.

Back in India, his work for independence was linked to his struggle for social change within Hinduism, especially the emancipation of the low caste 'Untouchables' (chapters 7, 8).

Gandhi's religious thought was based on the link between realising God (or *satya*) and serving others. It was a religious matter when people were ill-treated and oppressed. So his struggle, whether in the social or political arena, was basically religious.

6. Neo-Hinduism: godmen and nationalists

The fifty years since Gandhi's death have seen further profound changes in Hinduism. We mention here two major streams of Neo-Hinduism. We shall look at them more closely in chapter 3. They are changing the way many Hindus think about their religion.

The godmen

Gurus have been a part of Hinduism from the earliest period. But the last fifty years have seen a dramatic increase in their number and importance, both inside India and around the world. Gurus had been coming to the West throughout the earlier years of this century (for example Swami Yogananda, Meher Baba, Y. Krishnamurti). But the 'conversion' of the Beatles, followed by the hippy trail of young people going to India for enlightenment in the seventies, showed that the channels were wide open for a number of highly prominent spiritual leaders. They included Maharishi Mahesh Yogi (Transcendental Meditation), Guru Maharaj Ji of the Divine Light Mission (later discredited when he married his

American secretary), Bhagwan Osho Rajneesh (at one point the owner of ninety-three Rolls-Royces), Guru Mayi of the Siddha Yoga movement (followed by the singer Lulu), and A. C. Bhaktivedanta Prabhupada, founder of the International Society for Krishna Consciousness (ISKCON), better known as the Hare Krishna Movement.

The gurus have also been extremely influential within India. Satya Sai Baba is perhaps the best known of hundreds of modern gurus there. They have followers from all backgrounds and influence every aspect of life.[10]

The nationalists

Mahatma Gandhi was shot in 1948 because he seemed to be betraying Hinduism by his openness to Muslims. The man who shot him (Naturam Godse) was a member of a group called the RSS, the *Rashtriya Swayamsevak Sangh* ('National Voluntary Society'), which believed passionately that the glories of the motherland were essentially the glories of Hinduism. The movement, which has grown in the fifty years since Independence, is sometimes referred to as Hindu 'fundamentalism', but it is really Hindu **nationalism** – a desire to return to the spiritual and cultural values which made India great in the past and can make it great once again.

The RSS is a cultural and social organisation, not a political party. Its ideology is reflected in other cultural and educational bodies, such as the VHP (*Vishwa Hindu Parishad*), and in political parties like the *Shiv Sena* and BJP (*Bharatiya Janata Party*). The *Shiv Sena* ('Army of Shiva') is essentially a regional body, inspired by the Hindu warrior king Shivaji, who defied the Moghul emperors and established a successful dynasty. The BJP is a national party which has come to increasing prominence and power, especially in North India. Its basic political platform is 'Hindutva', the Hindu nation (chapters 3, 8, 9).

Reflection

There are different ways of looking at the story of Hinduism's development. One perspective sees many streams, with a great variety of cultural and historical influences. Another sees the whole as an organic growth from the very beginning of time.

Whatever the exact nature of its growth, Hinduism has shown a remarkable capacity to adapt to the changing environment, absorbing ideas from other backgrounds and synthesising them in new and surprising ways. This chapter describes some of the profound changes of the early centuries, while the last 100 years have seen the radical changes brought by figures like Vivekananda, Mahatma Gandhi, the gurus and the nationalists. We are still absorbing their impact.

The story of Christianity seems equally diverse, at first sight. The Bible contains many stories, stretching over a similar period. But running through them is one main story. It begins with God's dramatic act of creation, followed by the equally dramatic but disastrous act of human beings turning away from God, choosing their own way. The rest of the story is God's plan to restore the ruined creation. It all centres around the coming of Jesus Christ into the world. The history of the Christian church, with all its weaknesses and strengths, is always looking back to God's action in Christ. He remains the turning point. Without him, Christians would say, there is no story. The question that needs to be asked is whether that is a limitation or a strength.

1. A prayer to Ganesha, the elephant-headed god who is worshipped at the beginning of any enterprise.
2. D. S. Sarma, *Hinduism Through the Ages* (Bharatiya Vidya Bhavan, Bombay, 1989), p. 1.
3. Romila Thapar, *A History of India: From the Discovery of India to 1526,* vol. I (Penguin, London, 1966), p. 28.
4. There are great differences between scholars about the dates of events, people and scriptures. Some scholars give much earlier dates than we have given in this chapter.
5. K. M. Sen, *Hinduism: The World's Oldest Faith* (Pelican Books, London, 1961), p. 43.
6. *The Laws of Manu*, 1.30–33, trs. Wendy Doniger with Brian K. Smith (Penguin, London, 1991), p. 20.
7. From a hymn by Yamunacharya, around 1100 AD, verses 23, 24, 29.
8. From a hymn by Dadu (1544–1603).
9. D. S. Sarma, *Hinduism Through the Ages*, p. 16.

10. We cannot do justice to the gurus in this book. The best survey is Vishal Mangalwadi, *The World of Gurus* (reprinted by Cornerstone Press, Chicago, 1992).

3

Who is a Hindu?

'While it gives absolute liberty in the world of thought it enjoins a strict code of practice. The theist and the atheist, the sceptic and the agnostic may all be Hindus if they accept the Hindu system of culture and life ... what counts is conduct and not belief.' S. Radhakrishnan[1] (1927)

'What makes Hinduism so different from other religions is that there is no list of dos and don'ts. You are free to do what you want.' A Hindu woman (1996)

The Indian connection

Hinduism is inseparable from the Indian subcontinent, though it has spread far beyond India and is now the third largest religious community in the world.

The word *Hindu* came from the Persians in the fourth century BC. It was the same as *Sindu* (which they could not pronounce), the Indus River in the North-Western plains of India. The Muslim invaders, many centuries later, called the region *Hindustan*, the country of the people of Hind/Sind – the Hindus. In the eighteenth century, as the British and other Europeans began to discover more about the religion and the culture of the country, they coined the word *Hinduism*. It described the religions, beliefs, customs, culture and way of life of the peoples of India.

They used the word in this broad way. As a result, they linked together groups with very different beliefs and practices. In the previous chapter we saw the developments from Vedic religion, with its rituals and priestly control, to the philosophers, to popular Hinduism with temples, idols and *puja*, to *bhakti*, to sectarian movements, to reformers, to the modern gurus. Add to that the village and tribal traditions, and remember that all these different forms can co-exist side by side – and you realise that 'Hinduism' is a 'complex, pluralistic network of religions'.

Is there such a religion as Hinduism?

A vigorous debate is still going on. Some argue that Hinduism is an artificial concept, constructed by Europeans. It has been 'compounded and confused' with all the different varieties that we have mentioned. Therefore, they say, 'Hinduism' means nothing more than the beliefs, practices and culture of the different peoples of India. A Hindu can be defined as an Indian who follows these beliefs and practices.

Others argue that there is a coherence and unity within Hinduism that go back a long way. It is true that the scriptures and teachers of previous centuries did not use the words Hindu or Hinduism. They referred to their religion as *dharma,* or sometimes *Arya dharma,* 'the religion of the Aryans'. It was often called *Sanatana Dharma*, 'The Eternal Religion'. They recognised that its growth and development had been very varied but they did not think of it as haphazard. In fact, some Hindus describe their religion as the oldest in the world, revealed all at once to the ancient sages. Others are more cautious: 'Hinduism is more like a *tree* that has *grown* gradually than like a *building* that has been *erected* by some great architect at some point of time. It contains within it . . . the influences of many cultures, and . . . as much variety as the Indian nation itself.'[2]

Hinduism is like the banyan tree. Its branches spread out to form new roots, which then create new trunks. We should not underestimate the organic nature of Hinduism but neither should we forget its variety. That is what makes it a puzzle, at first sight. Hinduism is not static but changing and reinterpreting itself whenever the need arises. S. C. Dube comments: 'Hinduism, such as it is, is a loosely structured federation of faiths, rather than a faith . . . Birth and minimal cognitive participation are enough to identify one as belonging to the Hindu faith.'[3]

A sociological definition

Until very recently the most common definition of Hindu was 'a person born into a Hindu family', as Dube's comment above implies. In practice this meant a person from the Indian subcontinent (with some exceptions which we shall see below).

We can call this a sociological definition of a Hindu, which links religion very strongly with culture and family ties.[4] It implies that you are born into a particular community with its own cultural, social and religious traditions. That is where you belong and where you should stay.

We have already seen how closely Hindu belief and practice are linked to the family. Fulfilling your *dharma* within your family framework could be a definition of being a Hindu. It is a way of life.

The *Laws of Manu* laid down the outlines of this way of life in great detail. It was known as *Varnashrama dharma**. *Varnashrama* sums up the two basic features of Hindu social structure in its classical form. It is based on **caste** and clearly defined **stages** of life, with distinct roles for men and women. We look further at these stages in chapters 7 and 8.

Caste

Caste was a form of class structure, introduced (or accepted) in Hindu society during the Vedic period. We don't know the exact details of how it developed, but one of the words translated 'caste' is *varna**, which means colour. It suggests that the caste system, whichever way it actually developed, was a means for the lighter-skinned Aryans to establish a hierarchy above the darker Dravidians. However, the *varnas* were meant to be co-operative and inter-dependent, though with distinct roles. The origin of this social structure was described in a hymn of the *Rig Veda*, referring to the creation of the world from the sacrifice of the original man (*purusa**): 'When they divided the man . . . his mouth was the Brahmin, his arms were made into nobles, his two thighs were the populace, and from his feet the servants were born.'[5]

This creation myth established a divine order, not only for

the cosmos, but also for the social groups within it. The four
main divisions were:

Brahmins (priests)
*Kshatriyas** (nobles and warriors)
*Vaisyas** (merchants and farmers, some craftsmen)
*Sudras** (servants and agricultural labourers)

The first three castes were known as the twice-born, because
the males in these groups were initiated into the Vedic rites.
In this ceremony the boy received a sacred thread which he
wore across one shoulder.

The four *varnas* were reaffirmed in the *Laws of Manu*,
where they were said to emerge from the body of Brahma.[6]
In addition, there was a fifth underclass, outside the system,
referred to as the 'Untouchables' (chapter 8).

The other word translated 'caste' is *jati**. This refers to
smaller groups, based on inherited professions and occupations. There are about 3000 *jati* today. Each has its place
within the four major *varna* groups (and some in the fifth
group beneath it). It is likely that these occupational groupings grew up alongside the *varna* system and at some point
were integrated into it – a process which still continues,
as groups and sub-groups change their position in the hierarchy.

Caste is linked with ideas of pollution and purity. The
higher the caste the purer the individual. Pollution is measured
by such criteria as contact with dead animals, dirt and ef-
fluents. Some occupations would clearly be more polluting
than others. Distinctions were maintained through marriage
within the caste system (endogamy) and strict rules about
dining between members of different castes.

The Sunday edition of any Indian newspaper carries several
pages of 'matrimonials' among the classified advertisements
(see Fig. 1). Most of them specify the caste of the prospective
bride or groom (along with other desirable qualities such as
the right height, face, complexion, domestic ability, education, job and salary). A very few say 'caste no barrier'. Asian
papers in the Diaspora carry the same type of advertisements.

Fig. 1

> BRAHMIN match for Saraswati Brahmin, fair, beautiful, slim, 24/160, 5500, MSc, BEd. Teachress, father lecturer, Box KA-8294-CA
>
> A SUITABLE beautiful, vegetarian match required for a tall, handsome Mittal boy, 27/177/69 MCA System Analyst, working abroad, handsome salary. Correspond with biodata, horoscope. Box 83179-CA

The practice of caste has changed dramatically in the last fifty years (chapter 8). Many of the restrictions and taboos are now obsolete, especially in urban areas, where caste has become almost the same as class and a person's profession and economic status may compensate for lower caste origins. But all still know the caste they belong to. The caste system retains great power and is all-pervasive. It has been described as the 'fixed point' which enables the diversity of belief and practice to exist. Mahatma Gandhi campaigned relentlessly on behalf of the out-castes, and criticised caste divisiveness. 'Caste has nothing to do with religion,' he said. 'It is harmful both to spiritual and national growth.' But he still regarded caste as the essence of Hinduism: 'Varnashrama does attach to birth. A man cannot change his Varna by choice . . . I believe that if Hindu society has been able to stand it is because it is founded on the caste system.'[7]

Gandhi wanted to reform caste, not abolish it.

Diversity in Hinduism

The caste system was a means of bringing unity to the staggering diversity of Indian (mainly Hindu) society, both past and present. India has a population of nearly 900 million people, increasing by about eighteen million each year. There are eighteen major languages and hundreds of minor ones, some spoken by several million people. Hindu beliefs and practices have developed, over the centuries, in the interaction between people of different races, cultures, regions and separate kingdoms. 'In fact, one way to think about India is as a people and a land made up of a series of minorities. For

Hindu society itself is internally highly structured and diverse and pluralistic.'[8]

Scholars sometimes refer to 'the great tradition' in comparison with 'the little tradition'. The great tradition includes the worship of the major gods, while the little tradition reflects the worship of regional deities, village gods and local spirits, influenced by folk religion and tribal deities. Another contrast can be made between those who follow the authority of the Brahmin priests and the *Vedas* and those who follow other traditions and practices. We shall explore some of these further in chapters 4 to 6.

Agehananda Bharati, an anthropologist, describes three major types of Hindu religion in India:[9]

- *village Hinduism*, based on belief in local demons, spirits and magic practices – but with some observance of main-line festivals and practices
  80–84% (about 400 million people)
- *Vedic Hinduism*, led by the priests, scholars and ascetics
  13–15% (about 65–75 million people)
- *renaissance Hinduism*, followed by some urban, middle-class people, based on the gurus, missions and other spiritual leaders   3–5% (about 15–25 million people)

Much of the material in this book relates to the second and third of these groups, although the vast majority of Hindus are in the first group.

Many regard this variety as a source of Hinduism's strength. It is able to accommodate them within its fluid blending of spiritual images. Each of them represents 'fragments of the absolute spirit'.

Hindus in India
The exact number of Hindus within India today depends on the interpretation of the figures for the 1981 and 1991 Census of India (see Fig. 2). The religious classification is not very reliable. Since 1981 it has been based on the religion of the head of the household.

Fig. 2. Religious populations within India

Hindus	82.64%	about 700 million
Muslims	11.35%	about 100 million
Christians	2.43%	about 20 million
Sikhs	1.96%	about 16 million
Buddhists	0.72%	about 6 million
Jains	0.48%	about 4 million
Other	0.42%	about 4 million

One way to look at the major caste groupings is as a figure of a man with one leg shorter than the other (see Fig. 3):

Fig. 3. Major caste groupings in India

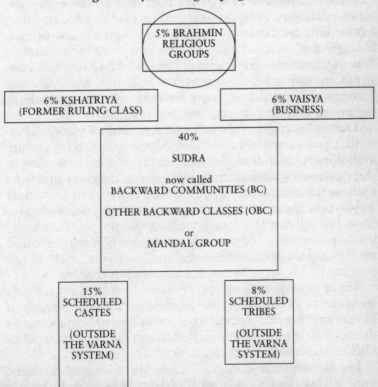

The largest group is the *sudras*, known today as 'Other Backward Classes' (OBCs). The three higher castes form only 17 per cent of the total population, while 23 per cent are from the Tribals and former Untouchables (officially known as Scheduled Castes because a schedule or list was drawn up in 1935). Though most of them are counted as Hindu in the census figures, it is an open question whether they would accept that description (chapter 8).

So the actual number of Hindus in India could vary from the 700 million of the census figures to around 500 million (if we remove the Scheduled Castes and Tribals), or somewhere in between.

Hindu expansion to South East Asia

Hinduism expanded into South East Asia in the early centuries of this era. You can still see the evidence today. Tourists to Bali are amazed to see Hindu temples and priests, festivals and processions. The exquisite temples at Angkor Wat in Cambodia are a unique blend of Hindu temple construction with local traditions. In Thailand, Malaysia and Indonesia you will find many Sanskrit words, especially in the vocabulary of religion, law and philosophy.

The whole region was influenced by Indian trade, colonisation and sometimes conquest. Along with it went culture and religion. Both Buddhist and Hindu missionaries went to these countries, with shifting influence at different times. As early as the first century AD, a Chinese traveller to Cambodia wrote that there were more than one thousand Brahmins from India living there and teaching the people. Cambodia was a powerful kingdom at that time. Later it was followed by Hindu kingdoms in Sumatra and then Java, with an important Hindu king, Sanjaya, in the eighth century.

There were flourishing universities which brought scholars from as far as China. As usual, there was a great variety of beliefs and practice, including the worship of some kings as divine, and the cult of Shiva-Buddha in Java, an example of Hindu-Buddhist syncretism.

Hindu influence continued until the thirteenth century, until it was largely replaced by Islam, at least in Indonesia and the Malay kingdoms. It is interesting that the Muslims with the most influence were Gujerati traders. India was still the dominant cultural influence in the region.

Nepal and Sri Lanka
To the north, the mountain kingdoms of Nepal were part of the Indian cultural region, though they were politically independent and were never part of British India. The majority of the people have been Hindu from the earliest period, but the Brahminical system was brought in around the fourteenth century. Nepal is a Hindu kingdom today, the only one in the world.

Hindus from India settled in Sri Lanka over a long period from the first to the fourteenth centuries. Another group migrated in the nineteenth century to work in the tea and coffee plantations on the eastern side.

Changing definitions
Although Hinduism had spread outside India, the sociological definition still applied. Whole groups of people had become Hindus and were incorporated into the Hindu social structure, by accepting the authority of the Brahmin priests and being incorporated into the caste system. They had become Indian by culture, if not by race.

When Gandhi left India for England at the end of the nineteenth century, he was still considered to be breaking caste by crossing the ocean. He could not fulfil caste requirements outside India. He could only persuade his mother to let him go by promising to abstain from contact with wine or women and never to eat meat.

But change was already taking place and Hinduism was poised to move out of India again, to become a world faith.

An ideological definition
Today anyone can become a Hindu, in a certain sense. Alongside the earlier sociological definition we can add an ideological definition: 'a Hindu is a person who adopts Hindu beliefs and practices, whether they are outwardly accepted into the Hindu community or not'.[10]

Not all accept this! Many still hold that 'you are born a Hindu and you will die a Hindu'. What lies behind these different views? We have already referred to some of the trends in chapter 2.

The discovery of Hinduism by European scholars. In the eighteenth and nineteenth centuries European scholars began to translate some of the Hindu texts and to excavate archaeological remains. Around 1850 the German Max Müller began to publish the monumental series of *The Sacred Books of the East*, opening up vast new fields of interest and study.

Selective adaptation by the West. Annie Besant arrived in India at the end of the nineteenth century and helped to develop the Theosophical Society, combining elements of Hinduism and Christianity in a pantheistic philosophy. It had links with the newly formed Indian National Congress and was sympathetic to its aspirations for independence. The Theosophical Society was important in disseminating Hindu ideas, both to Europeans and to educated Indians, inside and outside India. Young Gandhi, struggling to maintain his identity in cold, grey London, was tremendously influenced by coming across the Vegetarian Society in London (which converted him into a vegetarian by conviction). He read the *Bhagavad Gita* in an English translation by Sir Edwin Arnold and books by Madam Blavatsky and Annie Besant, all Europeans who had incorporated elements of Hinduism into their philosophy and religious beliefs.

Cultural and nationalistic export. Hinduism took a major step in transforming itself from an inward-looking to an outward-looking faith through the work of Swami Vivekananda, one of the leaders of the Hindu renaissance (chapter 2). In 1893 Vivekananda burst upon the world scene at the Parliament of World Religions in Chicago. His brief opening speech made a dramatic impact as he greeted his 'sisters and brothers of America' in the name of 'the mother of religions' and 'millions and millions of Hindu people of all classes and sects'. His simplicity and the persuasive message of the unity of all religions gained many followers. People were made aware of Hinduism as a powerful social and cultural force.

And Hinduism was being changed in both directions. As it responded to the challenges and stimulus of outside influences, it also prepared to preach its universal truth to the world.

Philosophical export. Following the work of Vivekananda, the Ramakrishna Mission established a number of centres outside India, presenting Hindu thought in ways that could be assimilated to Western thinking. It emphasised Vedanta and met considerable success, especially among writers and artists. *Vedanta for the Western World* was published in 1930 with contributions from Christopher Isherwood and Aldous Huxley. About the same time Sarvepalli Radhakrishnan, later the second President of India, became Spalding Professor of Eastern Religion and Ethics at Oxford University, where he gave a notable series of lectures published as *The Hindu View of Life*.[11] This was a clear and attractive presentation of Hindu thought, simply and coherently explained.

While Hinduism was becoming better known to many sections of European culture, its impact was still comparatively slight, confined mostly to a minority of intellectuals and artists. (This is not to underestimate the underlying influence of Hindu thinking on European culture over this period.) The situation changed dramatically from the 1960s. From then on we can identify four major groups of Hindus outside India:

A. *The gurus and their followers*
We have already referred to the stream of gurus from the 1960s onwards (chapter 2). The gurus made Hinduism accessible. Their focus was clear: on the guru as the authoritative spiritual guide. And their message was open to all: they rejected caste and other social hierarchies. The only requirement was to accept the guru and his message, usually with an initiation ceremony, which might include a *mantra* and a technique for meditation or *yoga*. They used English and were skilful in modern methods of communication, using speeches, music, books, leaflets, films, audiotape and videos. They incorporated Christian and other ideas into their teaching, arguing that all religions were equally valid, or could be

combined. They based this on Hindu notions such as the
unity of all spiritual experience, the importance of meditation,
the concepts of *karma* and *dharma* – and, above all, the need
for a guru.

Depending on your perspective, this whole movement of
the gurus outside India could be described as skilful communication or the commercial packaging of Hinduism. As a
young Hindu from Kenya comments: 'These days when there
is proselytising and short cuts to Nirvana by the gurus, it
seems easier to become a Hindu.'

The gurus have also been very influential in the next two
groups.

B. The New Age Movement
In her best-sellers *Out on a Limb* and *Dancing in the Light*,
Shirley MacLaine describes her previous incarnations and out
of body experiences. She passes on messages to humanity
from the beings for whom she became a 'channel', such as:
'If everyone was taught one basic spiritual law, your world
would be a happier place. And that law is this – Everyone is
God. Everyone.'

Shirley MacLaine is one of the best known advocates of
the New Age Movement. It is a rainbow of widely different
beliefs and practices. But its philosophical foundations are
Hindu, along with ideas from Buddhism, Jainism and other
Eastern religions. It also incorporates many of the spiritual
disciplines which are common to Hinduism and Buddhism,
such as meditation, different forms of *yoga*, and the
channelling of occult powers.

Some Hindu gurus have been popular with New Agers,
who have been willing to borrow ideas which appeal to them
from any source. The gurus fulfil a need by providing people
with a package put together according to their specifications
and requirements. We could call it 'designer Hinduism', in
which the guru sets out his boutique.

The concern for health and wholeness – so central to the
New Age Movement – is another area to which Hindu
philosophy and complementary medicine contribute. Deepak
Chopra, author of the best-seller *Ageless Body, Tireless Mind*,

was formerly associated with Maharishi Mahesh Yogi and TM. Now he runs the Chopra Centre for Well Being in California, promoting Quantum Healing. This harnesses mental energy to control the body in a state of health, so that you can live to a great age. Film star Demi Moore hopes to reach 130 by following his teaching.[12]

Deepak Chopra recommends workshops run by Jill Purdy in the UK, on 'The Healing Voice'. These teach *mantras* and sonic meditation, ways of breathing and producing sounds which enable you 'to set different parts of the body-mind in resonance' in order to 'heal and tune the *chakras** and subtle body'.

The Center for Eternal Values in Madras offers a cure for ME. Its founder, Mr Vydyanatha, does this by 'invoking the higher divine for which he becomes a channel'.

The New Age Movement also contains a group of 'self-religions', combining Eastern monistic spirituality with Western psychology. The basic aim is to discover the God within you – your Self. Deepak Chopra calls it 'the wizard within'. You can see this approach in some management courses which emphasise the unlimited potential within a person.

Hindus would find aspects of the New Age Movement hard to recognise. But it has certainly contributed to the spread and the growth of Hindu ideas at all levels, around the world (chapter 10).

C. *The Diaspora*

In 1971 General Idi Amin decided to expel the Asians from Uganda. Thousands arrived in the UK, from Uganda and other East African countries, with little more than the clothes they were wearing. As they established themselves in Britain, they joined many others who had come directly from India.

Indians had been emigrating over the last 150 years to different parts of the British Empire, such as South and East Africa, Central America, Fiji, and South East Asia. Most were Hindus, though there were substantial numbers of Muslims and Sikhs. In the early post-war years there were new waves of migration, caused partly by the violence following

Partition and partly by the need of countries like Britain for large pools of labour. The expulsion of the East African Asians in the early 1970s brought a substantial group of Hindu professionals to Britain. Around the same time, there was a lot of immigration to the USA from India, again mostly white-collar professionals.

The table in Fig. 4 shows the distribution of major communities of Indian origin outside India, though there are many other smaller communities. In most places the majority are Hindu.

Fig. 4. People of Indian origin outside India[13]

Sri Lanka	1,350,000	Trinidad	421,000
Malaysia	1,209,500	Fiji	326,015
South Africa	821,000	Burma	300,000
USA	815,447	Canada	200,000*
Gulf	800,000	Singapore	159,000
UK	675,000*	Netherlands	102,000
Guyana	500,000	East & Central Africa	100,000

There are also Hindu minorities in Pakistan and Bangladesh.

*Countries where Sikhs are a substantial proportion, up to 50%

Hindus in Britain

It is hard to obtain reliable statistics for the Hindu community in Britain. Figures range from 400,000 to 1 million (the lower figure is probably more accurate), of whom 70 per cent are Gujerati and 15 per cent Punjabi. There is an increasing number of Tamils from Sri Lanka.

As the Hindu communities have established themselves the larger community, they have maintained their Hindu identity, though with changes (chapter 8). Worship has always been associated with home and family, so it could continue without interruption. Every Hindu home would typically have its own temple or shrine (chapter 6). The East African Asians had already moved once before: they were used to carrying their gods and their worship with them.

Cultural associations

In many places an 'Indian association' would be the first organisation to be established, to provide for the social, cultural and religious needs of the community, including the celebration of festivals. (This happens in all the countries where Indians go. For example, in Konstanz, Germany, an Indian professor has established the Deutsch-Indgesellschaft as a cultural and social organisation.)

Next would be caste and sometimes ethnic associations. There were also informal groups called *bhajan** or *satsang**, that met for singing *bhajans,* devotional songs of worship (chapter 6). Worship might be conducted in any of these groups, or at some of the meetings of cultural and caste organisations.

Temples

Temples came somewhat later as official places of worship established according to Brahmin rites, with images brought from India and duly installed. Temples also function as places of community activity, including programmes for women, children, sports, language classes, yoga and meditation. The religious, social and cultural elements blend together, as always in Hinduism.

The gleaming marble temple at Neasden is the most visible symbol of Hinduism in the UK. It was built by one of the groups of the Swaminarayan Mission, funded entirely by donations from the community, including gifts of money, in kind and of labour. The marble was quarried in Bulgaria, carved in India by traditional craftsmen, and shipped to London, where an army of volunteers put it all together. The images were installed in August 1995 and in March 1996 Prince Charles was invited to visit the temple and to take part in its worship. He has been followed by other notable figures, including Prince Philip and Tony Blair.

Other UK communities are planning temples, including a group of doctors from Andhra Pradesh in South India who want to build an even bigger temple, modelled on the great temple to Lord Venkateshwara at Tirupati. It is scheduled for completion in 1998, one of the major projects funded by the Millennium Commission.

Gurus
Some of the *bhajan* or *satsang* groups are linked to a particular guru, mostly those whose followers are almost entirely Indian, especially Swaminarayan and Radha Soami.

A few gurus attract both Indian and non-Indian followers, particularly Satya Sai Baba. The Satya Sai Baba Council of the United Kingdom recognises eighty to ninety groups, with both Indian and non-Indian members. Some meet in temples while most meet in homes. Shri Mataji's Sahaja Yoga Meditation holds eight groups a week in London and twenty-eight more around the country.

ISKCON, with twelve major centres, attracts mostly non-Indian devotees. But Bhaktivedanta Manor in Hertfordshire, the movement's main centre for training, donated by Beatle George Harrison in 1973, has become a focus for much wider activity. Like any Hindu association, it was freely used for worship as well as for training. Controversy arose when the annual festival to celebrate the birth of Krishna (*Janmashtami*) began to attract thousands of visitors, resulting in conflicts with the local villagers of Letchmore Heath. The conflict came to be seen as an issue of religious freedom for Britain's Hindus. Permission was finally granted in May 1996, on condition that an adequate road be constructed to keep traffic from the village.

The National Hindu Students' Federation, established in 1991, with over 3000 members, aims to deal with issues facing British Hindu youth, such as 'identity, marriage, Hindu rituals and symbols, caste discrimination ... More current and controversial topics include the threats of religious conversion and the Kashmir problem.' The fifth Anniversary Ball was a black-tie affair at the London Hilton – an indication of the social group it is aiming for.

D. *The nationalists*

Chanting in unison, young boys and old men march before their garlanded gods. Faintly incongruous in a place of worship, their stiff movements and lilting voices are a cross between religious devotion and army drill.

'We come here to do exercises and offer prayers to the motherland,' said Bharat, 13. 'We learn why we are uniting as Hindus and why we are proud to be Hindus.'

The room, blooming with tinsel, coloured lights and luminous idols, could be in India's Hindi heartland. But this meeting is taking place in a quiet residential street in Ilford, east London. Every Wednesday night the local '*shakha*', or branch of the Hindu Swayamsevak Sangh (HSS) meets. The HSS is an offshoot of the right-wing Hindu nationalist movement, the RSS, which campaigned against Muslims in the run-up to Indian independence in 1947.

Cadres come to the Ilford temple to exercise and pray. Every week there is a discussion on Hindu nationalism. Tonight the Ilford *shakha* is celebrating. The BJP, the political party spawned by the RSS, has emerged the winner in the Indian election.[14]

The HSS aims 'to provide and propagate Hindu thoughts, ideals and values of life ... We are uniting Hindus and teaching them their history ... Rootless immigrants will have no value anywhere' say its leaders. It works chiefly among Hindu youth, with over 100 branches in the UK.

The HSS in the UK reflects the politics of Hindu nationalism in India. When a mob destroyed the Babri Masjid mosque in December 1992, there was violence, not just in India but around the world, where Hindus and Muslims from the subcontinent clashed.

The Hindu nationalists are a minority, but with increasing significance. Romila Thapar, the Indian historian, describes them as '*syndicated Hinduism*'. While some feel that it is healthy to link Hinduism with India's cultural heritage and national prestige, others feel that in the long run it is contrary to Hinduism's traditions of tolerance and non-violence.

Reflection

Who is a Hindu? The answers show astonishing diversity – from illiterate villagers to Nobel prize-winners, from East African business people to Hollywood entertainers. (In this book we have not done justice to the beliefs and practices of the vast majority in the villages.)

What holds them together? Until recently the answer was clear: the social structure of family and caste. Today Hindu ideas seem to have permeated the modern world much more widely than its social structure. Take Hollywood as an example. Many of its films reflect Hindu ideas, from *Star Wars* (based completely on a Hindu and Buddhist world-view) to *Hello Again* (reincarnation) or *The Secret Garden* (the world in Krishna and Krishna in you).

What does this mean for Hinduism? Can it receive people of such different backgrounds into its social and cultural framework? 'Yes!' say some. 'Probably not!' say others.

Like other major faiths, Christians have also wrestled with these questions. Jesus was Jewish and so were his first followers. But they rapidly included people of diverse cultures and races, including Indians, from the first century onwards. Today Christ's followers come from almost every nation and culture in the world. Europeans and North Americans are outnumbered by the peoples of Africa, Asia and Latin America. The only qualification should be acceptance by Christ, not cultural requirements. But the churches face the constant challenge to allow the 'good news' to be expressed in changing cultural forms.

1. *The Hindu View of Life*, first published 1927. Reprinted 1993 (HarperCollins India, New Delhi), p. 52.
2. K. M. Sen, *Hinduism: The World's Oldest Faith* (Pelican Books, London, 1961), p. 14.
3. Quoted by Gerald Larson, *India's Agony over Religion* (State University of New York, Albany, 1995), p. 82.
4. This definition is based on Agehananda Bharati, quoted in a survey by C. V. Mathew in *Neo-Hinduism: a Missionary Religion* (Madras, 1989).
5. *Rig Veda* 10.90.11.
6. *The Laws of Manu* 1.31.

7. Quoted by Sunder Raj, *The Confusion called Conversion* (TRACI, New Delhi, 1988), p. 107.
8. Rajni Kothari, quoted in Larson, p. 177.
9. Quoted in Larson, pp. 20–21.
10. Based on Agehananda Bharati.
11. See note 1, above.
12. *Telegraph Magazine*, 25 May 1996.
13. These figures are from different sources.
14. *The Observer*, 19 May 1996.

4

Sacred Texts

The root of religion is the entire Veda;
Families rich in Vedic verses join the highest
   rank;
A twice-born man who recites the Veda attains
   perpetual, unending happiness;
The eternal teachings of the Veda sustain all
   living beings.[1]

Bangalore Airport, Sunday morning: '*Indian Airlines an-*
nounces the departure of its flight to Pune. Will passengers
please proceed to the security check . . .'

The announcement was barely over. As the passengers
began to pick up their hand-baggage, they were waved back
to their seats by airport staff. The luggage conveyor stopped
moving. There was an expectant silence. And then on the TV
monitors, all over the airport, the flight information disappeared and instead came the familiar figures of Rama and
Sita. It was 9 a.m., time for the weekly instalment of
Ramayana. All over India people settled down for the next
half hour. The airport staff were not going to miss the serial
either. And the passengers for the Pune flight had to wait.

For over two years the magic continued, as Doordarshan
(Indian TV) broadcast the *Ramayana* and *Mahabharata* and
the whole of India remembered the glories of its two great
epics.

Stories have always been the traditional way into the
Hindu scriptures. The vast majority of Hindus know parts
of their scriptures through the stories they have *heard* – from

their parents, grandparents or a village storyteller – or *seen* –
in films, acted out at festivals or in comics. Today they can
also see them on TV, video or CD-Rom. Several leading
Indian politicians are former film stars, previously seen and
adored by millions as heroes or even gods from those stories.

A minority have also studied the ancient scriptures which
lie behind the stories. Like everything else connected with
Hinduism, the Hindu scriptures are vast and varied. We may
be used to the idea that the Bible is a library of books (sacred
to Jews, Christians and Muslims). The Hindu scriptures are
a library of libraries.

The *Vedas*

The earliest collections have the most authority, though they
are less familiar to the average person. They are known as
the *Vedas*. The word means 'knowledge' or 'insight' (from
the same root as 'video'). The *Vedas* are the basis of orthodox
Hindu belief and practice. 'Back to the *Vedas*!' was the slogan
of the nineteenth-century *Arya Samaj* reformers (chapter 2).

The *Vedas* are a vast collection of hymns, stories, rituals,
magic and philosophy, composed and ultimately written
down over a period of centuries.

The *Vedas* in the broad sense include three major groups
of collections (see Fig. 5). We can call them the work of **poets,
priests** and **mystics**, though there are elements of all three in
each group. Sometimes the first group alone are referred to
as the *Four Vedas*.

The *Vedas* are known as *sruti** ('heard'). In other words,
these sacred texts are eternal and were heard by scholars
directly from God. Both their form and content are sacred. It
is believed that the *sound* of the texts, the spoken words, is
as important, if not more so, than their meaning.

A. *The Poets*
The earliest collection is the **Rig Veda**, or 'Songs of Praise'
(composed around 1500–1000 BC).

The *Rig Veda* contains over 1000 sacrificial hymns

dedicated to different gods and the elements of nature. They give us a clear picture of early Vedic religion, mostly reflecting the beliefs and practices of the Aryan settlers, though there must have been a gradual fusion with elements from the culture of the indigenous peoples.

The hymns are sung to the gods as if they were present in the form of natural forces, the powers that affected and controlled people's lives. There were clear connections with the Indo-European pantheon. The oldest of the gods was Dyaus Pitri, the 'Heavenly Father/Sky Father', corresponding to Jupiter or Zeus. But he was much less important than Varuna (Greek Ouranos/Uranus), who was also god of the Sky and guardian of the cosmic order and morality. Around him were many other gods, divided into the three spheres of their primary activity:

- *gods of the sky*, such as Surya (sun), Savitri (the sun's life-giving power), and Usha (dawn)
- *gods of the atmosphere*, such as Vayu (wind), Ratri (night), Rudra (a god with vaguely defined powers over nature)
- *gods of the earth*, such as Agni (fire), Yama (death)

The storm god, Indra, one of the gods of the atmosphere, became steadily more important, first alongside Varuna and then replacing him.

The hymns reflect the life of the Aryans. The gods ride into battle in their swift chariots to fight demons or the enemies of the Aryans. They drink the life-giving juice of the *soma** plant. And they depend on sacrifice.

Sacrifice was fundamental to the Vedic religion. As we saw in chapter 2, the focus gradually shifted from the gods to the sacrifices themselves. They were believed to have power to order and control events in the world, including the gods. From this insight there were two developments:

Fig. 5. The major texts of the Hindu scriptures

THE *VEDAS*	*Sruti* – Heard Texts of supreme authority	Approximate dates[†]
A. The Four *Vedas*		
Rig Veda	hymns to the gods, cosmology sacrifice	1500–1000 BC
Yajur-Veda	sacrificial formulae, which detailed the performance of rituals	
Sama-Veda	priestly chants and melodies to accompany the hymns and rituals	
Atharva-Veda	spells and charms (*mantras*) used by the priests	900 BC
B. The *Brahmanas** and *Aranyakas*	speculation on the nature of the sacrifice; reflections on mental performance rather than the rituals	800–500 BC 400–200 BC
C. The *Upanishads*	mystical and esoteric texts on the nature of spirituality, consciousness and knowledge	700–200 BC
OTHER SCRIPTURES	*Smriti* – Remembered Texts of popular belief and practice	
The Epics		
Mahabharata	the story of the Pandavas and Kauravas, conflict of good and evil, other stories and parables	300 BC–300 AD
Ramayana*	the story of Rama as an example of obedience to good moral conduct (*dharma*)	200 BC–200 AD
The *Puranas*	mythological exploits of the gods. 18 major *Puranas*	300–1500 AD
The *Laws of Manu*	books of moral and social law attributed to Manu, the first man	200 BC
The *Sutras*	short texts taken from the teachings of sages, set out in easily learnt verses	
Bhagavad Gita	poem included in the *Mahabharata*; a summary of beliefs about God and the ways to salvation	500–200 BC (some believe up to 200 AD)
Tantras	ritual texts including *mantras*, spells and ways of meditation	600–700 AD
Bhakti Songs of Devotion	personal worship songs	600–1500 AD
Commentaries	texts explaining earlier scriptures and arguing theological and philosophical positions	700 AD–present day

[†] *There is great variety in the dates given by scholars, especially for older texts. The dates given here try to reflect this. Some scholars give much earlier dates than the range above.*

The search for the underlying principle behind all reality.
Among the many gods, Indra is worshipped the most. Other
gods are identified with Indra. The idea is beginning to
develop that he represents the Absolute Spirit, although he is
not the Absolute himself. The hymns of the *Rig Veda* also
contain speculation about the origins of the world. Some of
it is very sophisticated, like the famous poem on page 79
(chapter 5).

The search for the correct rituals to control all reality.
While some speculated about the origins and meaning of life,
others sought to control it through the rituals of the sacrifice.
The role of the priests became more and more important.

B. The Priests

The increasing power of ritual and the priests is reflected in
the later hymns of the **Rig Veda** and the three other collections
that grew up alongside it:

The *Yajur-Veda*: a collection of sacrificial formulae, which
detailed the performance of rituals, over which the hymns of
the *Rig Veda* would have been sung.

The *Sama-Veda*: a collection of priestly chants and melo-
dies to accompany the hymns and rituals in the sacrificial
performances.

The *Atharva-Veda*: a magical text, which details the spells
and charms (*mantras*) used by the priests. Throughout this
period, the rituals grew in power, complexity and abstraction.
The priests were the ones who knew the rituals and their
significance. So they controlled the spiritual direction of the
Hindu people.

The second major group of collections reflects the same
focus. The **Brahmanas** (800–500 BC) were priestly manuals
concerned with communal and family sacrifices. They were
texts for the Brahmin priests, which investigated the rituals
and began to form speculative theories about the magic
invoked in them. For the sacrifice to be effective, the ritual
actions and words must be absolutely correct and the procedures had to be followed exactly.

For example, the *Satapatha Brahmana* expounds the belief
that the priests themselves were the ones who could ensure

order, rather than the gods, who were after all dependent on the sacrifices for their energy.

The *Brahmanas* were followed by a collection called the *Aranyakas*, 'The Forest Treatises' (about 400–200 BC). They focused on the rituals and sacrifices but began to move behind them. The rituals themselves were not the source of power, they said. The mind of the individual performing the ritual was more important. Mental performance could accomplish the outcome, instead of physical practice. Uri Geller, bending spoons on TV, or Luke Skywalker with his Jedi mind-tricks, seem to have tapped into the same kind of psychic powers! In the Scottish Highlands, whole villages sometimes have 'the second sight', a psychic ability to read thoughts and see people who are absent.

The *Aranyakas* are still concerned with the power to control, to get results. But they have started on the journey inwards which reached its climax in the third major group of the *Vedas*.

C. *The Mystics*

'. . . those forest Sages began everything; no fundamental problem of philosophy, nothing that has disturbed the schools of controversy, escaped their notice'.[2]

The *Upanishads* are perhaps the most influential Hindu texts in the West. They are a collection of philosophical and mystical dialogues, written by travelling sages of the period (between 700 and 200 BC). They are also known as the *Vedanta*, the 'end of the *Vedas*'. There are at least 108 texts, although only about ten to fifteen are considered really significant. *Upanishad* means to be 'sitting down near', referring to the practice of tuition at the foot of a spiritual leader. These tutorials took place in the forests, where the sages wandered alone, met other sages, argued spiritual and philosophical issues, and instructed willing disciples in the knowledge that they had gained.

The *Upanishads* moved behind the gods of nature and the tradition of ritual and sacrifice, perhaps drawing on an alternative mystical tradition from the people of the Indus Valley Civilisation. They searched for the one underlying reality, a spiritual reality more real than the physical reality that we experience every day.

Experiments in consciousness

One of their distinctive features was the focus on the Self and the nature of consciousness. What makes up our personality? What is the connection between different states of consciousness – waking, dreaming, dreamless sleep? Who or what is common to each state, or knows each state?

Modern theories, based on the analogy of physics, refer to 'thoughtons' as the smallest unit of the energy expressed in thought, like 'protons' or (old-fashioned) 'electrons'. The sages of the *Upanishads* were exploring the same territory, over two millennia ago. They experimented on the different states of consciousness, through meditation and other techniques, concentrating on the internal process of thinking itself. They concluded that there is a real self at the core of our being, which remains whether we are awake, sleeping or dreaming, in this world or another world.

> When we wake up from a dream, we do not pass from unreality to reality; we pass from a lower level of reality to a higher one ... In meditation ... when concentration is profound, there are moments when you forget the body entirely ... A body becomes like a comfortable jacket: you wear it easily, and in meditation you can unbutton and loosen it until you are scarcely aware that it is on you at all. Eventually there comes a time when you get up from meditation and *know* that your body is not you.[3]

The Ultimate Reality

So the *Upanishads* celebrated the discovery of the Self, the innermost essence of a person. But they went further. They believed that this Self, or innermost essence of a person, is identical with the innermost essence or One that lies behind all reality. That One is called **Brahman**. The Self is called **Atman**. *Atman* is identical with *Brahman*. Our real Self is the same as the Ultimate Reality, God.

This is the central insight of the *Upanishads*, expressed in their most famous statement – 'Tat tvam Asi', 'You are That'. In modern terms it is like saying that 'I' am essentially pure energy. And that energy is the same as the energy behind all matter and existence. They are all inter-connected. We are all inter-connected. 'I have become a vibration . . . a wave in this big ocean, a small particle in this cosmic all,' says Neera Kapur, an Odissi dancer from Kenya.

Life beyond life

If the Self is the ultimate reality, it must be eternal. This leads to the other great innovation of the *Upanishads*. The Self does not live only once. When a person dies, the Self departs to another life:

> As the caterpillar, having come to the end of one blade of grass, draws itself together and reaches out for the next, so the Self, having come to the end of one life and dispelled all ignorance, gathers in his faculties and reaches out from the old body to a new.[4]

What is the basis on which the Self moves from one body to another?

> As the person acts, so he becomes in life. Those who do good become good; those who do harm become bad . . . As we act, so we become.[5]

This is the belief in **reincarnation** or the transmigration of souls, and the law of *karma*, cause and effect in the moral realm. There is no evidence of this belief in reincarnation based on *karma* in the earlier literature of the *Vedas*. It was almost certainly an innovation by the philosophers of the *Upanishads*, dating perhaps to around 700 BC. But by the time of Buddha and Mahavir, it had become accepted as common doctrine.

The contribution of the *Upanishads*

The *Upanishads* are the foundation of Hindu religious thought and philosophy. D. S. Sarma sums them up: 'The

gods recede into the background, the priests are subordi-
nated, sacrifices are looked down upon, contemplation takes
the place of worship and the acquisition of divine knowledge
takes precedence over the performance of rites and ceremonies.'[6]

Stories of the Gods

The *Vedas* have always had the highest authority for Hindus.
But the majority have had little access to them. For one thing,
they were in Sanskrit. Until recently only Brahmins would be
expected to study them. It would take a young man twelve
years to memorise them and learn to recite them properly,
with the correct intonation and understanding. Even hearing
them was restricted to the three higher castes. It was forbidden for a *Sudra* to listen to the *Vedas*. Women were also
excluded. Pandita Ramabai, a Brahmin's daughter, was a
remarkable exception at the beginning of this century, because
her father taught her Sanskrit and encouraged her to study
the scriptures.

There were other scriptures that were more accessible to
the average person. They were in the category called *Smriti**
– remembered. They were not considered to be eternal like
the *Vedas* but were sacred texts, with great impact.

The epics
The epics of Hinduism are the **Ramayana** and the **Mahabharata** (see Fig. 5). Both were communicated orally for
generations and only printed in the nineteenth century.

Mahabharata
The *Mahabharata* is the longest poem in the world at nearly
100,000 verses. It is a story of family rivalry and affairs of
state. The Pandavas and the Kauravas come into conflict after
a gambling contest, in which the oldest son of the Pandava
family stakes and loses the kingdom to his Kaurava cousin.
After thirteen years' exile the Pandavas return to reclaim their
land. Splitting the allegiances of the kingdom, the two families

fight. In the epic battle, the Pandavas are advised by Krishna. The battle wipes out all but the five Pandava sons, and they take control of the land. Yudhishtira rules for many years before abdicating and taking his brothers and Draupadi, the brothers' wife, to the Himalayas in search of heaven.

The narrative is not so simple, however, as it contains numerous interpolations of a spiritual nature, and many sub-plots. The most important addition is the *Bhagavad Gita*, a relatively short poem containing a dialogue between Arjuna, one of the Pandava brothers, and Krishna. The *Bhagavad Gita* is arguably the most influential text of Hinduism. We shall look at it more closely below.

Apart from this, the *Mahabharata*'s major contribution to Hinduism is its representation of a popular religion, rather than the élite practices of the *Vedas* and the ascetic mysticism of the *Upanishads*. The *Mahabharata* is full of gods and heroes, local spirits and demi-gods. Brahma the creator, Indra the storm god and Vishnu are the primary deities. The inter-action between the gods and human beings and the ways in which they all behave, provide spiritual and practical lessons for all. There are stories of kings and wise men, ordinary people and animals. Many are retold in a popular series of comics, *Amar Chitra Katha*. From them children learn lessons like hospitality, duty and the right conduct for each class of person.

Ramayana

The *Ramayana* is much shorter than the *Mahabharata* (24,000 verses) and recounts events believed to have taken place earlier. Rama, the central figure, is the seventh *avatar* (or incarnation) of Vishnu (Krishna is the eighth). Rama, heir to the throne, is exiled with his wife Sita and brother Lakshmana, following a deal between his father and step-mother. Sita is abducted by the demon Ravana and taken to Sri Lanka, forcing Rama to wage war on the demons and rescue her with the help of a monkey army. The story ends with Rama's return to the throne and the tragic banishment of his wife, as the people question her chastity while she was a prisoner. Though he believes in her innocence, Rama

banishes her in order to please the people. In the final chapter
Rama finds his wife with his two new children, long afterwards, and discovers her true identity. Sita is the daughter of
the Earth Goddess, to whom she returns.

Their impact

Both epics have been recited, sung and acted out across India
and beyond, over many generations. Today schoolchildren
around the world learn the story of Rama, as they study the
festivals of different cultures, especially *Diwali* (chapter 6).

The epics have had tremendous impact on popular
religion, especially the *Ramayana*. The story of Rama is a
story of *dharma* and high ethical standards (chapter 7). Rama
is the ideal of heroic manhood, suffering and triumphing.
Sita is the ideal woman, accepting her role within Rama's
dharma, loyal to him even when her purity is questioned,
suffering injustice in silence.

Both epics illustrate the moral and spiritual truths of the
Vedas. The characters are ideals for us and the stories have
deeper philosophical or moral meanings, underlining the
distinction between good and evil.

The Puranas

The *Puranas*, 'Stories from Ancient Times', follow on from
the epics. They contain stories of the gods and heroes, presenting Hindu thought and philosophy in popular form. The
main *Puranas* dealt with five major themes:

- The creation of the cosmos.
- The re-creation of the cosmos after its periodic destruc-
  tion and re-absorption.
- The genealogies of gods and sages.
- The ages of the world and their rulers.
- The genealogies of great kings.

They also contained information about festivals, caste
obligations, pilgrim sites and stories of the gods. The *Puranas*
were really 'A plain man's guide to popular Hinduism' or
'Everything you wanted to know about the gods but were

afraid to ask'. Some tried to weave together the different mythologies and traditions. Others emphasised devotional practices and moral examples of *dharma*.

There were eighteen major *Puranas*, each linked to one of the three major deities, Brahma, Vishnu and Shiva (chapter 5). Some represented the perspective of a particular sect, including practices and ideas which were not approved by the Brahmins. Popular Hinduism was strongly influenced by the *Puranas* but the later reformers felt that they contained excesses of superstition and strange practices.

The Laws of Manu

While the epics and *Puranas* told stories to illustrate spiritual and moral truths, the **Laws of Manu** spelled out a *system* to order every detail of daily life. This was *dharma* codified, as we saw in chapter 2. It was composed around the second century BC and was one of the first texts to be translated by the British, who needed it to understand and take over the legal system of the land.

The teachings of wise people

The *Sutras* were short pieces believed to have originated from the teachings of influential sages. Perhaps the best known in the West is the *Kama Sutra*. They dealt with particular elements of the *Vedas*, such as ethics, ritual law and *dharma*. They were split into three groups, the *Dharma Sutras*, the *Srauta Sutras* and the *Gryha Sutras*. The different systems of Vedic thought were presented in easily learned verses which enabled students to grasp the larger picture through short passages. They were like textbooks for the first steps in religious teaching. Later commentaries were based on them.

The Bhagavad Gita

The *Bhagavad Gita* (The Song of the Lord, The Divine Song) is probably the most influential of all the Hindu scriptures, known and loved by millions. It is a small part of the massive *Mahabharata*, added at some point, probably between 500–200 BC.

The setting is a battlefield. Arjuna, the Pandava leader,

faces the moral and spiritual dilemma of having to kill his
relatives and friends in the battle. Krishna, his charioteer,
instructs him. What begins as a lesson in *dharma* turns out
to be something much more.

The greatness of the *Gita* and the secret of its attraction is
that it clearly brings together the different strands of Hindu
beliefs and practice up to that time:

Is God one or many, impersonal or personal? Krishna
accepts the concept of the One behind all the manifestations.
But he does not stop with an impersonal deity:

The Lord, O Arjuna, is seated in the heart of all beings,
causing by His divine power the entire cosmos
to revolve as if mounted on a machine.
Take refuge in Him with your entire being, O Bharata;
by His Grace you will gain supreme peace and the eternal
  abode.[7]

More than that, Krishna instructs the worshipper to focus
everything on him:

Fix your mind on Me, be devoted to Me,
Sacrifice to Me, bow to Me and to Me shall you come.
This is my pledge to you, for you are dear to Me.
Abandon all *dharmas* and take refuge in Me alone.
Fear not, I will deliver you from all sin.[8]

So God is portrayed as a personal presence, Krishna, who
can be loved and related to. But he is also universal, greater
than the entire universe, as he reveals his divine nature as
Vishnu in a vision with 'the splendour of a thousand suns
rising simultaneously in the sky'.[9]

What about the different ways to salvation? The *Gita*
resolves any conflict between them. All are good. All can be
practised. But again, Krishna goes a step further. The best
thing is to focus all the ways on him:

Whoever offers me a leaf, a flower, fruit or water with
  devotion,

that offering of devotion from the pure in heart I accept.
Even if a very wicked person worships me exclusively
he should be considered righteous, for he has rightly
   resolved.[10]

*How do you combine detachment from the world with
involvement in it?* Krishna recommends a way – the path of
action without desire, or selfless action *(nishkama karma*)*.
This becomes a key ethical concept, which we shall return to
in chapter 7.

What about the social order? The *Gita* re-affirms the traditional social order with the fourfold division of castes and
stages of life (chapters 7, 8).

The *Gita* is a masterly synthesis which millions have followed as their guide. Some scholars feel that its synthesis
contains contradictions, since the different ways and perspectives are not the same. They argue that the different parts
reflect different backgrounds rather than one composition.
Whatever the history of its construction, those who put it
together in its final form felt that the best way was to combine
the different views.

Arthur Basham, a well known scholar of Indian culture,
points out that the *Gita* answers many of the questions from
a similar framework to Christian theology.[11]

Songs of Devotion

The *bhakti* movements produced their own texts, songs composed in the languages of the people, not Sanskrit (chapter
2). Some were erotic poems of human love, while most
focused on the devotion of the worshippers to God. The
bhakti scriptures spoke to people's hearts. It was said of the
sixth-century Alvars that they 'sang the Buddhists out of
South India', a short while before Sankara's rigorous argu-
ments sought to demolish their philosophy. In the fifteenth
century Tulsidas retold the story of Rama in Hindi. The
Ramayana of Tulsidas was the same outward story as the old
epic but was really a poem of devotion to a personal God,
incarnated as Rama. It had tremendous influence.

Commentaries

Sankara, Ramanuja and other scholars expounded their teaching by writing commentaries on the major texts of the *Vedas*, giving their own authoritative interpretations. In recent years gurus like Sai Baba, Rajneesh and A. C. Bhaktivedanta Swami Prabhupada, the ISKCON leader, have spread their views through commentaries and sermons, lavishly produced and printed in thousands around the world. They are also available on audiotape and video.

The Scriptures Today

Some people use small collections of scriptures for their daily prayers. They may contain wise sayings from various sources, or prayers to one of the gods.

Understanding the scriptures isn't always easy. The *Gita* is influential but some find it difficult. Who explains it to you?

'That's where you need a guru,' says Ranjana, a Delhi housewife, enthusiastically. She finds Murari Bapu the most helpful, though she has also tried two or three others. They are all available on video, to buy or hire from the local video shop. 'He explains it all so beautifully. When he tells you that the Ganga is our mother, you feel it's like waves going over you.'

A London businessman explains that the way to interpret is to look for the spiritual meaning behind the stories: 'Hinduism is complicated as it got mixed with mythology and artistic licence. It's educated people's responsibility to separate them and educate others. Say for example, Goddess Kali in her violent temperament tramples over her own husband Lord Shiva. It's a parable, meaning anger is detrimental to one's welfare.'

If you are serious, you can join one of the *Gita* study groups which are beginning to spring up. Or you can now get the *Gita* on floppy disk – or as part of a new spiritual rock opera on CD.[12]

For some the interpretation is not so important. They believe that the *sounds* of the scriptures have power, for example when recited by a priest. They also recite verses and phrases as *mantras*. These are combinations of syllables, usually taken from the *Vedas* and taught by a guru. When a *mantra* is 'received' in this way from the mouth of a guru, it has great power. It can activate vibrations, arouse divine energies, or produce a 'super-conscious' state of feeling. Every Hindu god is represented by a *mantra*, so reciting it draws the power of that god into a person.

In the past, children automatically absorbed the stories and traditions from their elders. Today more systematic efforts are made to teach them, especially in the Diaspora. In the USA, children go to summer camps where they act out the old stories from the Ramayana and Mahabharata and learn about Hindu culture. In the UK, a group in Leicester sends teams each weekend to other cities to teach Hindu families, so that they don't lose their hold on the scriptures of their heritage. At the Swaminarayan Temple in Neasden, 800 young people come together each Saturday evening for classes on moral and spiritual issues.

In Leicester the local newspaper, the *Leicester Mercury*, has articles at festival times, telling the stories behind them and explaining their meanings. *The Hindu*, a national newspaper published in Madras, has always had a daily religious column, explaining a text or story. Now it is available on-line, around the world.

Reflection

The scriptures have always been important for Hindus, though not always accessible. The situation has sometimes been similar to the medieval church in Europe, which confined the Bible to Latin and only allowed the priests to read or explain it. Even they were mostly ignorant of its contents. When the Bible was translated into the language of the people and given its due authority, it released power and light into the lives of ordinary people, as they read and responded to God's truth.

What is the core of the Hindu scriptures? People give different answers. For some Hindus today the scriptures are still seen as magical texts, in which sound and ritual and correct recitation are most important. Others look to the gurus to give meaning through

their discourses, in person or on tape or video. Outside India the
Upanishads are the most influential, while within India the *Gita*
appeals to educated people. For ordinary people the stories of the
epics and *Puranas* are the most influential.

1. *The Laws of Manu* 2.6; 3.66; 4.149; 12.99.
2. W. B. Yeats, *The Ten Principal Upanishads* (Faber and Faber,
    London, 1970), p. 11.
3. Eknath Easwaran, *The Upanishads* (Arkana Penguin Books,
    1988), p. 23.
4. *Brihadaranyaka Upanishad*, III.4.3.
5. *Brihadaranyaka Upanishad*, III.4.5.
6. D. S. Sarma, *Hinduism Through the Ages* (Bharatiya Vidya
    Bhavan, Bombay, 1989), p. 6.
7. *Bhagavad Gita* 18.61–2.
8. ibid., 18.65–6.
9. ibid., 11.12.
10. ibid., 9.26,30.
11. Arthur Basham, *The Sacred Cow: The Evolution of Classical
    Hinduism* (Rider, 1989), pp. 93–4.
12. *The Song Divine – A Spiritual Rock Opera*, to be produced by
    Gita Productions, Zurich.

5

Fundamental Beliefs

Ekam sad viprah bahudha vadanti
Truth is one, though the wise call it by many names.[1]

Hinduism is concerned with the fundamental questions that we all ask. *What is the meaning and purpose of life? Where do we come from and where we are going?*

In other words, like all religions, it asks questions about God, ourselves, and the world in which we live. As we try to answer these questions, we will keep referring to six key words that give a summary of Hindu belief – *Brahman, atman, karma, sansara, dharma, moksha*. Along with them we can add **caste**, which holds together the Hindu social structure. (We shall look more at caste in chapters 7 and 8.)

God

God is the centre of Hindu belief. There are many names for God – not just for individual gods like Vishnu or Shiva – but for God, such as *Bhagwan, Ishwara, Parmeshwar, Narayan* or *Brahman.*

Every type of view about God (including atheism) can be found in Hinduism. This is partly because of the long period of historical development, and the mixture of beliefs from different regions, cultures and races. Instead of rejecting one belief in favour of another, Hinduism has absorbed and synthesised them. This is its unique ability. K. M. Sen described Hinduism as 'a great storehouse of all kinds of religious experiments'.²

Developing ideas about God

We begin by looking back at the early period. In chapters 2 and 4 we saw something of the progress of beliefs:

From the Creator God to the gods. We saw that the *Rig Veda*, the earliest collection of hymns, already reflects belief in many gods. There are hints of an original creator God and worship through sacrifice, along with the search for the One who unites the different forces. Increasingly the attributes of the gods are concentrated on Indra, the storm god. This search might perhaps have led back to monotheism. But it was overshadowed by another development.

From the gods to the sacrifice. The sacrifices and rituals became more and more important. Behind them lay the belief that what was done in the rituals reflected the larger order of the cosmos. Magic and astrology were also ways to control events. Some referred to *rta** as the ordering principle of the universe.³ Others speculated about creation, concluding that the gods were part of creation rather than distinct from it. All these ideas led in a direction away from monotheism.

From the sacrifice to the One. The *poets* of the *Rig Veda* were groping toward the realisation of the One. D. S. Sarma describes them as 'the most astonishing record of the march of the mind of man from the worship of the half-personified forces of Nature like fire, wind and rain to the realisation of the Absolute Spirit, of which we, as well as the world with which we are surrounded, are only broken fragments'.⁴

The *priests* were preoccupied with rituals and the control they sought. The *philosophers* and *mystics* continued to search for the One unchanging reality behind the changing world. They discarded the personal gods of polytheism. And they were not satisfied with outward rituals. They looked inward, through meditation.

The result of their search is called **monism**. This begins from the assumption that there is only one eternal principle in the universe. There is no Creator God above and separate from the creation (the view which is called *theism*). Instead there is the Absolute, the One behind all reality, the 'One without a second', whom they called Brahman.

God beyond attributes

How do you describe this God? As soon as you start giving attributes and using adjectives like good, powerful, compassionate, you bring God into the realm of differences. The best we can say is that God is *neti, neti* 'not this', 'not that'. The Supreme Being is *Nirguna* Brahman*, 'beyond attributes' and indescribable. It is transcendent and impersonal but at the same time one who 'is seated in the secret cave of the heart' of all beings.

> That which is invisible, ungraspable, without family,
>   without caste,
> without sight or hearing, is It,
> without hand or foot, eternal, all-pervading, omnipresent,
>   exceedingly subtle.[5]

'The best description of God in Hindu thought is energy,' says Professor Bikhu Parekh, of Hull University.[6] 'When I dance, I feel the energy of the cosmos flowing through me,' says Neera Kapur, an Odissi dancer from Kenya.

God with attributes

This absolute, impersonal God may be manifested to us in different ways, which include the personal. These manifestations can be described as good, powerful or compassionate. This is *Saguna* Brahman*, 'Brahman with attributes', also called *Isvara*.

Advaita

This monistic view is the idea of God in the *Upanishads*. Buddha, Mahavir and the atheists (chapter 2), were also part of this search, away from outward rituals and the pantheon of gods. Centuries later Sankara (chapter 2) strongly re-affirmed this view of God as the only Reality. He argued that there could be no duality, no alternative principle in the universe – so his philosophy was called *advaita*, 'non duality' or 'absolute monism'.

It is also known as *advaita Vedanta*, because it is based on the 'end of the *Vedas*'. *Advaita Vedanta* has been made popular in the West through scholars like Dr S. Radhakrishnan and movements like the Ramakrishna Mission and the Chinmayananda Mission.

Modified monism

But not all have accepted this strong statement of impersonal absolute Brahman. Quite apart from popular religion, philosophers also struggled to reconcile this with their experience of reality, especially the two other philosophers, Ramanuja and Madhava. Their views are presented below in very simplified form.

Ramanuja (about 1100 AD) was a worshipper of Vishnu and a leader among the *Alvars* ('the divers into God'). He wrote commentaries on the same texts as Sankara, arguing a different position. God is like the soul within the world. The self is bound by ignorance and needs to be released by knowledge and meditation (as Sankara had said). But knowledge is not enough. We need the grace of God in response to the devotion of the worshipper.

Ramanuja's followers split into two famous schools of thought about God's grace. The *cat school* believed that the worshippers were totally dependent on God's grace, like a kitten carried by its mother, hanging helpless by the scruff of its neck. The *monkey school* believed that the worshipper must also play a part, like a baby monkey clinging tight to its mother's belly.

Ramanuja's system was called *vishishtadvaita**, 'modified non-duality' or 'modified monism'. It is a more common view among those who follow monism than the 'absolute monism' of Sankara. When John Robinson, Bishop of Woolwich, wrote his famous book *Honest to God* in 1963, he used the word 'panentheism' to describe one of his ideas about God – God is in everything. It is really the same as Ramanuja's 'modified monism'.

Madhava (about 1200 AD) went still further to declare the distinction between God, the world, and the soul. Salvation is by the grace of God to the worshipper. Madhava's view is called *dvaita** or 'duality'.

Fig. 6. The differing views of Sankara, Ramanuja and Madhava

Absolute monism	Modified monism	Dualism
advaita	*vishishtadvaita*	*dvaita*
non-duality	modified non-duality	duality
Sankara	**Ramanuja**	**Madhava**

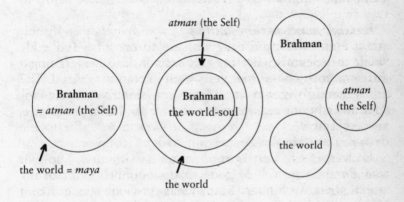

God is the only Reality	God is like the soul in the world	God, the world and the Self are each real and distinct
The world appears to be real but by comparison with God it is unreal (*maya*)	The world and the Self are like the body. They have some separate reality but are dependent on God.	
The Self is already one with God, but is trapped by ignorance. It needs to realise its unity in order to be liberated.	The soul enters union with God by grace, based on knowledge and devotion.	The Self enters relationship with God by grace. Each individual Self retains its identity.

A personal god?

Whatever their ultimate philosophical ideas, it is true to say
that most Hindus, most of the time, believe in God as in some
sense personal. They worship the One God in many different
forms, which can be confusing to the newcomer. People are
free to select one or more deities on whom they focus their
devotion, their *ishtadevata**. Some see the god on whom they
focus as *the* God, whom they worship in an almost monotheistic way. Many in the *bhakti* movements have been like
this. Some worship the Mother Goddess or feminine principle
– a distinct stream within the Hindu framework. There are
also regional and local gods connected to a particular place.
The variety seems bewildering, until we remember that each
can be linked in some way to the others.

One God, many manifestations

Most Hindus give primary worship to one or a few gods,
while they acknowledge the existence of the others. Ultimate
reality is one – but it manifests itself in countless ways. Each
is valid in its own way, for its own situation. We cannot limit
God to only one manifestation at any particular time, place
or perspective.

A key word in this connection is ***roop**** (form or aspect). A
god can take any form or *roop* to suit the situation. The epics
and *Puranas* are full of gods appearing in all kinds of dis-
guises, divine or human. Many village gods are seen as a *roop*
of one of the greater gods. An idol is the *roop* of the god it
represents. Certain human beings may be regarded as a god
in human form: 'Tulsidas [a poet saint] was a *roop* of *Shiva*.
That's how he got the power to compose the *Ramayana*,'
explained one woman as she described the background to
the epic.

The gods

Three of the gods are universally acknowledged as leaders –
Brahma, Vishnu and Shiva.[7] They are often described and
sometimes portrayed as the *trimurti** (three images), in-
dicating that together they represent only one reality. They
are the creator (Brahma), preserver (Vishnu) and destroyer

(Shiva). Brahma's role has virtually disappeared and there is only a single temple to Brahma in the whole of India. Vishnu and Shiva are the two most powerful deities, worshipped as supreme by almost equal numbers of followers. Both have inspired intense devotion.

Vishnu the protector

Vishnu is thought of as preserver and protector. He is often depicted as lying on the coils of the cosmic serpent and sometimes linked with creation, in place of Brahma. He is also worshipped very widely through his incarnations or *avatars* (see below). Those who follow Vishnu are known as *Vaishnavites**.

Shiva the powerful

Shiva is the most enigmatic of the great gods, with many facets. Many believe that the origins of Shiva worship go back to pre-Aryan times. Shiva is often portrayed as an ascetic, with matted hair, smeared with ashes, a deadly snake round his neck and the sacred river Ganges flowing from his hair. He is also portrayed as Nataraja, Lord of the Cosmic Dance of the universe. The image of the dancing Shiva is one of the most famous works of art. All this symbolises his mysterious, unbound power and energy, which can both destroy and create. The most important symbol of Shiva is the *lingam**, the male organ, expressing the creative force behind the universe.

Although he appears fearsome, Shiva is easy to please and generous to his worshippers, who are known as *Shaivites**.

Other major gods

Brahma, Vishnu and Shiva have their consorts – **Saraswati**, **Lakshmi** and **Parvati**. Other gods are part of their families, like **Ganesha**, the elephant-headed son of Shiva and Parvati. Ganesha is particularly popular as he removes obstacles and brings good luck. No journey or project should begin without worshipping Ganesha. **Hanuman**, the monkey god, one of the heroes of the *Ramayana*, is also very popular – resourceful, helpful and kind. **Murugan**, another son of

Shiva, is worshipped by many in South India. In East Ham the London Sri Murugan Temple is a focus for the Tamil population there.

Lakshmi, the goddess of wealth, plays a key role in the *Diwali* festival, when every business closes its accounts and starts the new financial year. Some time during the day (preferably after the close of business) a priest visits each shop or business. The family members crowd into the small room where the cash and accounts are kept. The *Diwali* lamps are lit and the priest recites prayers to Lakshmi in Sanskrit, while the old account books are closed and the new ones opened. Each page is blessed and marked with '*OM*' in red powder. A gold coin may be offered in worship, symbolising Lakshmi, who is invited to come and bring prosperity. Then sweets are distributed and everybody enjoys the rest of the festival.

As we saw in chapter 3, the vast majority of Hindus are in the villages. They worship *regional and village gods* who represent local powers, often seen as guarding the people of that place. Many of them are linked to the 'national' gods and identified as their local *roop* or representative. For most village people – and others – *demons and spirits* are also very relevant and powerful. In fact, much of their worship is at this level of placating spirits, seeking protection from illness and accident, and praying for prosperity in their fields.

Avatars

One way in which the gods manifest themselves is through their incarnation or *avatar*, the 'descent' of a god in human or other form. The best known are the ten incarnations of Vishnu, of whom the most important are Rama and Krishna, the focus of the majority of *bhakti* movements.

Krishna explains the purpose of these incarnations: 'Whenever righteousness declines and unrighteousness arises, then I manifest myself upon the earth. For the deliverance of the good, for the destruction of evil doers and for the re-establishment of righteousness, I am born from age to age.'[8]

Krishna the lover

Krishna is unique in the devotion that he has attracted from
Hindus of every generation and almost every background.
Krishna is the central figure of the *Bhagavad Gita*, who links
together all the strands of Hinduism up to that time in a
masterly synthesis. But Krishna's popularity is based much
more on the stories about him in the later *Bhagavata Purana*.
They tell of his miraculous birth and his upbringing as a
cowherd to protect him from enemies. Several *bhakti* movements focused on Krishna, the lover who was somehow
accessible to the human soul. His exploits with the milk-
maids, especially Radha, were seen as the symbol of love
between the human soul and God. We can see a parallel with
the portrayal of love in the Bible's Song of Solomon.

The Mother Goddess

A distinct stream is the worship of the Mother Goddess,
known as *shakti* (power), *Mataji* (Mother), or simply *Devi**
(The Goddess).

Devi destroys the wicked buffalo demon Mahishasura. The
gods are helpless to overcome this demon, who can only be
killed by a woman. Finally they combine to produce a new
being representing all their most powerful attributes. She is a
dazzling sight, radiant with beauty, riding on a lion and
burning with anger against evil. After her victory, the gods
themselves pray to her: 'Great Mother, through your grace
the trinity carries on the functions of creation, protection and
desolation. You are all pervasive and everything in creation
is part of you. Saints who realise your subtle, secret presence
attain unshakeable peace and understanding, through
meditation.'[9]

Behind this story lies the belief in the feminine principle,
shakti, the highest form of beauty and energy, as a key principle of life and the universe. It is frequently combined with a
male god, especially Shiva. That represents the union of male
and female, the symbol of the most potent force in the universe.
Shiva is represented by his *lingam* and this is frequently found
together with the *yoni** – the male and female organs together.

Devi is identified with Parvati, Shiva's consort, or with

other great goddesses like *Durga** and *Kali*. Each village also
has its own goddesses, manifestations of the Mother Goddess.
They are considered to be very powerful, controlling diseases
like smallpox, the fearful killer of just thirty years ago.

Prayer to *Mataji* is very effective. The feminine principle
expresses the fertility of a woman, the provision and protection of a mother. She is loving but can also be fierce. Only
Devi can deal with the demon. Kali is the most famous
expression of the Mother Goddess – terrible with her necklace
of skulls, her animal sacrifices and blood running everywhere.
But she is loved and adored by her worshippers.

Worship of the Mother Goddess is sometimes expressed as
shakti worship, linked with a special type of *yoga* called
tantra yoga or *shakti yoga* (chapter 6).

The Self

Who are we? The basic answer of the Hindu tradition is not
confined to human beings. In each of us there is the essential
Self, the innermost essence, the ***atman***. And the Self is the same
in a man or woman, child or puppy, an elephant, tiger or ant.[10]

As we saw (chapters 2 and 4), the philosophers of the
Upanishads searched for ultimate reality by examining their
own consciousness. Through their meditation they found the
Self (*atman*) within themselves. They concluded that this
principle or power was also the ultimate reality behind the
whole universe. So the same life force pervades human beings,
animals, and every part of the universe.

The Self is not identical with body or mind. It is a free
state of eternal existence, called *sat**. It has true self-consciousness – *chit**. When a person becomes truly aware of
this (for example through meditation or ecstasy) it leads to a
state of pure bliss – *ananda**. So the nature of the essential
self is *sat-chit-ananda* or pure existence, pure consciousness,
and pure bliss. And this is Brahman, the Supreme Reality.

But life in practice is not *sat-chit-ananda* – far from it!
Why? What is the nature of our everyday existence in the
real world?

The World

What is the world and where does it come from? There are
many answers, in stories, myths and philosophical descrip-
tions. An early poem in the *Rig Veda* shows a very modern
uncertainty about the whole process:

When even nothingness was not, nor existence.
There was no air then, nor the heavens beyond it.
What covered it? Where was it? In whose keeping?
Was there then cosmic water, in depths unfathomed?

Then there was neither death nor immortality,
nor was there then the touch of night and day.
The One breathed windlessly and self-sustaining.
There was that One then, and there was no other.

At first there was only darkness wrapped in darkness.
All this was only unilluminated water.
That One which came to be, enclosed in nothing,
arose at last, born in the power of heat.

In the beginning desire descended on it –
that was the primal seed, born of the mind.
The sages who have searched their hearts with wisdom
know that which is kin to that which is not.

And they have stretched their cord across the void,
and know what was above, and what below.
Seminal powers made fertile mighty forces.
Below was strength, and over it was impulse.

But, after all, who knows, and who can say
whence it all came, and how creation happened?
The gods themselves are later than creation,
so who knows truly whence it has arisen?

Whence all creation had its origin,
he, whether he fashioned it or whether he did not,
he who surveys it all from highest heaven,
he knows – or maybe even he does not know.[11]

Here various causes are suggested for the origins of the universe – *desire, strength, impulse, heat*. Other hymns suggest *speech* as the fundamental principle.[12] A famous passage describes *sacrifice* as the beginning of it all. In one hymn it is the sacrifice of *purusa*, the Primal Man.[13] In other places this cosmic sacrifice is the sacrifice of *Prajapati**, the Creator.

In one popular account, Brahma creates from a vast egg, floating on the cosmic waters. These represent the elements of the universe, which have already evolved from the original matter. From the egg, Brahma separates three worlds of earth, atmosphere and heaven and fills them with living creatures, wise people and gods. Then he sustains the world as Vishnu the preserver. Finally he destroys it as Shiva.

The time between creation and dissolution is called a 'day of Brahma'. This contains four major cycles (*yugas**), each of which lasts millions of human years. The fourth is *kali yuga*, which is the worst. Conditions in the *kali yuga* are terrible – and we are now in it! Parents often refer to this to explain to their children why things are so bad these days. At the end of his day Brahma sleeps and the world is dissolved. When he wakes the world is recreated for another billion-year 'day of Brahma'.

In all this speculation there is a search for order and principle. It is assumed that the universe is basically there. The gods are part of the existing order, not its originators. It is not actually creation – the universe evolves or emanates from its basic substance.

What is the world made of?

One of the major schools of philosophy is called *Sankhya**. This starts from two fundamental realities: *prakriti** – matter, and *purusha* – consciousness. When these come in contact, creation takes place and the world unrolls in twenty-five stages. All matter consists of three qualities called *gunas**, like three strands of a rope. They are *sattva** (goodness or purity), *rajas** (energy or passion), and *tamas** (inertia or dullness). These were originally in equilibrium, but as the world evolves they form different combinations. Everything else, including our outer body, physical and mental, is derived from these qualities. So our actions and characters are a mixture of them – depending on the balance in each person.

How real is the world?
In the *Sankhya* philosophy, both *prakriti* and *purusa* are real. So our world, which has come into being from them, is also real.

Sankara put forward a different view. For him *Brahman* was the only reality, and everything else in the universe, except the *atman*, was unreal by comparison. He used the word *maya* to describe this, translating it 'illusion'. As a result, it is widely considered that Hindus see the world as illusion, *maya*. This is one view, but not the only one. Other philosophers, like Ramanuja, used *maya* to mean the creative power of God.

Modern Hinduism reflects an ambivalent view of the world. It is accepted as real because of our experience and because of modern science. For Jawaharlal Nehru, the first Prime Minister of India, science and industry were the great hope for the future. He described the factories and heavy industrial plants of the fifties and sixties as the 'temples of modern India'. But the world is ultimately unimportant because the true spiritual reality is not in the world.

How real are we?
In some schools of thought the outer self, physical and mental, has a distinct identity. It is really real. For others it is ultimately unreal. But all agree that what is most important is the inner Self. Because of ignorance, or selfishness, we do not realise who we are and what we can become. Many Hindus speak of the problem of the *ego*, that outer self which keeps coming in the way, binding us to this life and keeping us from realising our true Self. In one tradition:

Maya means *prakriti* (primary matter).
It is the basic substance and the cause of all bondage.
It is the cause of ego and attachment to the body and its relations.[14]

'I want to lose my ego, I want to lose my pride and become part of this loving, creative Being,' says Neera Kapur.

Where does it all lead?

We need to be liberated, whether in this life or later in the cycle. The ultimate goal is to escape from this body, the outer self.

How? This is where we come back to the most basic beliefs. Behind the gods are the actual forces that control the universe, principles like *karma* and *dharma*. They determine what happens to a person.

All agree that the real Self – *atman* – is eternal. Is this the same as the soul? Some distinguish between *jiva**, the individual soul, and the *atman*, while others describe them as more or less the same. Some refer to the *paramatman**, the 'supreme soul', which is the same as the Supreme God.

The Self – *atman* – progresses on its way through the cycle of birth and rebirth (*sansara*), which is controlled by the law of *karma*. This determines the nature of the next birth and the length of the cycle. Everybody has to pay their 'karmic debt'. 'We live in accordance with our deep driving desire. It is this desire at the time of death that determines what our next life is to be. We all come back to earth to work out the satisfaction of that desire.'[15]

Almost all Hindus believe in *karma* and *sansara* and agree that the ultimate aim is release or liberation from the cycle – *moksha*.

What does *moksha* mean?
For some, *moksha* means freedom from any connection with the world of change and appearance. It is literally being alone. There is no God, just the soul, alone.

For others, *moksha* means absorption into Brahman, like a drop in the ocean. Neera Kapur describes it as like becoming 'a wave in this big ocean, sort of merged in this cosmic world . . . I am just a small particle. And yet I am like a microcosm in this macrocosm. I feel unified with this.'

For others, knowing God implies a distinction and aware-
ness of one's own identity. Ramakrishna said that he wanted
to 'taste sugar, not just become sugar'. In the Swaminarayan
tradition the redeemed soul (*jivatma*) continues to serve and
worship God, who remains 'separate and supreme above
all'.[16]

How do you achieve *moksha*?
The *Gita* sums up three major ways, which each have their
place:

- The way of knowledge – *jnana marg*.
- The way of devotion – *bhakti marg*.
- The way of action – *karma marg*.

We could add to these

- The way of sacrifice and ritual.
- The release of power – *shakti*.

We shall see in the next chapter how these are worked out in
worship and practical daily life.

When can you hope to reach *moksha*?
In the classical tradition, the Hindu man goes through four
stages of life (chapters 3, 7). Very few reach the fourth stage,
when they give up everything for the spiritual life. If they do,
this could be an indication that they are nearing the end of
the cycle of birth and rebirth. A few have that conviction
even earlier on. Shivraj was told about the great rejoicing
when he was born. His mother had had two miscarriages
and his aunt had lost her child. His birth was seen as very
auspicious. He had been born a boy, born a Brahmin, after
so much misfortune. He and his family were convinced that
he must be on the verge of *moksha*.
    Those who are ready for *moksha* do not return to the cycle
of birth and rebirth: 'But not those who are free from desire;
they are free because all their desires have found fulfilment in
the Self. They do not die like the others; but realising

Brahman, they merge in Brahman.'[17]

Some believe that certain people gain so much special merit (*punya**) by their good actions that they go to heaven (*swarga**) for a while to enjoy its blessings. But it is only temporary and they come back to continue the cycle of birth and rebirth. Others who behave very badly may go to a corresponding place of punishment for a while. 'But the large majority of humanity do not belong to either category and are only a mixture of ordinary *punyas* and ordinary sins. This large majority of people are born again in this world.'[18]

Many simply believe that their loved ones have gone to 'heaven'. It's common to read a death notice like this in the newspaper: 'Our beloved mother left us on 14th January to go to her heavenly abode. We will never forget her loving example.'

Some people are believed to obtain release while still living in this world, through their complete detachment from the things of this life. They are known as *jivanmuktas**, the ones who are 'liberated while still alive'. The *Upanishads* describe their state:

> He who is not inwardly touched by exhibitions of joy, jealousy, fright, anger and greed is said to be a *jivan-mukta* ... He in whose inward vision there are no likes and dislikes, and who conducts himself as if in a state of sleep, is said to be a *jivanmukta* ... He who has given up righteous as well as unrighteous conduct ... is said to be a *jivanmukta*.[19]

Rabi Maharaj's father, who followed the way of knowledge (*jnana*) and meditation, entered into a state of living realisation, a few weeks after his marriage to Rabi's mother. He sat in this state, beyond communication with ordinary people, for eight years until one day he left this life. He had already entered *samadhi**, total absorption like a trance.

Those who follow the way of devotion may find themselves 'in direct and ecstatic union with God', an unmediated experience of God. But for most people, their aim is to follow the way that has been set for them, to practise their *dharma* (duty) and hope to move at least a step forward, rather than backward.

At a funeral the priest recites these words from the *Bhagavad Gita*:

Just as in this body the embodied self has childhood, youth
　　and old age,
in the same way it gets another body; the wise man is not
　　confused about that.
Just as a man abandons his old clothes and puts on new
　　ones,
the embodied self abandons its old bodies and goes on to
　　new ones.[20]

Reflection

Trying to summarise Hindu beliefs seems a bewildering task. There is such variety! Perhaps the simplest way is to go back to those six key words – *Brahman, atman, dharma, karma, sansara, moksha* – though even they convey a wide range of meanings.

When we look at Hindu ideas about *God*, it is easy to find similarities with Christian beliefs, as well as differences. After all, Hinduism is 'a great storehouse of all kinds of religious experiments . . .' *(K. M. Sen)*. Perhaps there are more differences when we look at views of the *Self* and the *world*. The world is basically there: it does not have a clear beginning, nor is it thought of as essentially different from God or Ultimate Reality. In the same way there is no clear dividing line between the inner Self and God. In fact, if we follow the most common interpretation of the *Upanishads*, they are identical. Some find this approach attractive and surprisingly modern. Others find that it leaves unresolved questions.

There is one question that we have hardly referred to in this chapter: 'What is wrong with the world? What is the basic problem?' We shall look at that question in chapter 7. But it is perhaps not accidental that it hardly appears here and seems less important. Christians emphasise the serious nature of sin and its damaging effects. (We shall try to explore what that word *actually* means in chapter 10.) Hindus on the whole are less troubled by that. Their concern is more with the debt of *karma* and how to fulfil their role in the cosmic framework of *dharma*.

1. *Rig Veda* 1.64.66.
2. K. M. Sen, *Hinduism: The World's Oldest Faith* (Pelican Books, London, 1961), p. 37.
3. Pronounced *ritta*. It can also be spelled *rita*, like the name.
4. D. S. Sarma, *Hinduism Through the Ages* (Bharatiya Vidya Bhavan, Bombay, 1989), p. 6.
5. *Mundaka Upanishad* 1.1.6, from R. E. Hume, *Thirteen Principal Upanishads* (Oxford, 1931), p. 367.
6. Speaking on the BBC World Service in July 1991.
7. *Brahma* should not be confused with *Brahman*, the Absolute, ultimate Reality.
8. *Bhagavad Gita* 4.7–8.
9. R. K. Narayan, *Gods, Demons and Others* (Mandarin Paperbacks, London, 1990), p. 63.
10. *Bhagavad Gita* 5.18.
11. *Rig Veda* 10.129.
12. *Rig Veda* 1.164.
13. *Rig Veda* 10.90.
14. *Shikshapatri* of Swaminarayan, 106.
15. *Brihadaranyaka Upanishad*, IV,4,6.
16. *Akshar Purushottam Upasana* (Swaminarayan Aksharpith, Ahmedabad, 1995), p. 156.
17. *Brihadaranyaka Upanishad*, IV,4,6.
18. V. Krishnamurthy, *Hinduism for the Next Generation* (Wiley Eastern, New Delhi, 1992), p. 2.
19. *Mahopanishad*, II.42–62; *Anna-purnopanishad* V. 14–22.
20. *Bhagavad Gita* 2.13.22.

6

Spirituality and Worship

OM bhur bhuvah swahah
Tatsavitur varenyam bhargo devasya dhimahi,
dhio yo nah prachodayat

We meditate on God's splendour and divine light
God is everywhere and in all beings
We pray for purity of mind and knowledge of the truth[1]

Acts of Worship
Early morning. As the sun rises, millions of Hindus are at
prayer. Some may have gone to a nearby river or pond to
bathe. Their prayer may include an invocation to the sun as
it rises. Most would pray at home.

The home
In a typical Hindu home the day begins with a regular
routine. In India, or wherever the climate permits, somebody
pours water on the *tulsi** plant in the courtyard. Then the
family members gather at the shrine which is found in every
Hindu home. The women and girls will all be there; the boys
and men may not always attend. Somebody opens the holy
book. Somebody else lights an *agarbathi* incense stick. The
gods are woken up, sometimes with a bell. They are washed
with milk and then covered with a cloth. There is a reading
from one of the books, the *Gita*, *Ramayana*, or a small
collection of scriptures, relating to one of the gods. Somebody
performs *arti** – an offering of fire before the gods. It could
be just a candle or a smouldering wick, but usually it is a

lamp on a tray, with fruit, flowers and grain, which is waved in front of the gods. Prayers are recited. The gods and the worshippers receive a daub of coloured paste or powder on the forehead.

In the evening, there is a similar routine. In some homes, whenever food is cooked, a portion is offered to the gods by touching it to their lips.

Apart from this family worship, many have their own individual routine, reciting prayers or reading from one of the scriptures.

Hindu prayer and worship begin from the home and the individual. Each family has its shrine, cared for mostly by the women of the family. It may be a separate room or an alcove with pictures or statues of the gods, small or large, depending on the family's devotion and resources. The images are of one or more gods on whom the family has a particular focus.

Temples
Every Hindu home is a temple and place of worship. But temples outside the home also play a significant role. They are the homes of the images of the gods, who are cared for and honoured there. Outside India, temples have also developed a significant role as community centres.

Temples range from small wayside shrines, or even a painted stone under a tree, to magnificent buildings which are works of art, some built over centuries.

There is no necessity to go to a temple, unlike some faiths where community worship is important. Some people visit the temple once a year, or on special occasions like festivals or weddings. Others go every day, especially if it is nearby. Many families go on a particular day, set apart for the god whom they worship: 'Monday is Lord Shivas's day. Tuesday is for Hanuman, Thursday for Lord Vishnu, Friday for Santoshi Maa. Rama and Krishna can be worshipped any day.'

What happens at the temple?
'When you go in, the first thing is to take off your shoes, out in the compound. Then you ring the brass bell, then go into the inner sanctuary to offer your worship, throwing petals or rice or a coconut or whatever. What happens at the temple depends on your purpose. If it is just a routine visit, you can ring the bell, sit for a few minutes or stand in an act of worship and quiet: then go to the inner sanctuary. This has other images inside and there is a priest there. He will call you and you bow to him and he will bless you and give you some *prasad** [the food which has been offered to the gods and given to the worshippers]. Then there is *jal* [holy water] – you are given a few drops of that to drink. The ritual varies – if you are going there in preparation for a marriage or something like that you would do different things. It's a very personal thing. You may have a big burden on your mind and you want to give a gift to a priest. There is a place to collect the offerings. There are different images in different places and individuals go at their own pace with no set pattern or routine.'

Although people worship along with others, they are essentially worshipping as individuals. It is not really corporate worship, as in some other faiths. 'You do things in a more organised way,' was the comment of some Punjabi policemen who came to a Christian church service in Pune. It is only recently, in the Diaspora, that temples are organising corporate times of worship, particularly at the weekends. At the big Neasden temple, Saturday evening is set aside for an act of community worship and teaching. In Southampton the times of the main *arti* are advertised outside and people come in groups for the main Sunday morning worship, followed by lunch together.

Images and worship
What place do the images play in worship? What is their significance? Hindus answer in different ways. The word for image is *murti**. It could be a picture, or a statue of any kind, from a rough piece of clay to an exquisite marble carving.

For some, the image is only a symbol, a pictorial representation of the unseen and spiritual. 'God is quite abstract. When I try to think of him I need some focal point to concentrate on', says Shanti.

Many regard image worship as an aid for those who need it. Sarita explained it like this:

'There are stages in worshipping God. I think a person sitting in front of the image is focusing his own image on the stone and getting it all channelled and charged up and re-focused back on himself. It's like feedback. This is the beginning; then you go higher and perhaps by learning other stages you reach just an abstraction, meditating on your self and on nature and becoming a part of them, a part of the whole thing. It's not that one is good or bad, but all of us evolve from one stage to another.'

But for others the image has power. When images are drawn or carved the different poses represent the qualities and characteristics of the gods. It is very important that these are drawn correctly. For example, the many arms represent the manifold power of a deity. By correctly representing the qualities of the deity, those qualities are available to the worshipper. The image is identified with the power of god it represents.

When an image is created, the final act is the 'opening of the eyes'. Every detail is complete, except the pupils of the eyes. When they are painted in, with the recitation of scripture by a priest, that is the moment when the spirit of the god enters into the image.

The images attract great reverence. When the worshippers care for them – by washing them, dressing them, feeding them – they are showing honour and respect. *Arti*, the fire offering, is an act of worship to a king. The images represent the gods as kings, with their own territory and subjects. Most temples have festivals when the images are taken out in a procession, around their territory. In Puri the image of Jagannath (Lord of the world) is taken out in a huge car with massive wooden wheels. Hundreds of people compete for the honour of pulling the Jagannath car. In previous times some would actually throw themselves under the wheels to be crushed as a sacrificial offering. The British inability to pronounce words properly has given us the 'Juggernaut', mostly now used of monster lorries on the M1 motorway.

For many Hindus, especially in villages, belief in spirit powers is very real. They use various devices to ward off magic spells or the evil eye, including lucky numbers, charms and amulets. It is considered unlucky to praise a new baby, for example, in case that attracts the evil eye. Buildings under construction have a mask or scarecrow figure hanging on them to keep it away.

Prayer

How do Hindus pray? Rajesh remembered what he was taught as a boy:

'We used to repeat a prayer which was taught from childhood. It began like this: "*Hey pati parameshwara* . . . O Lord God . . ." We repeated that prayer, or there was a *mantra* which we were taught, OM *Namah Shivai* – an invocation to Shiva. Whenever you faced exams or a difficult situation, you were told to say this mantra 108 times and that was a magic number. You would find a corner somewhere and repeat it. I can remember borrowing some beads and using them to pray the right number of times. At the morning prayer time there was a holy book in our shrine and whoever got up first would open it and that would be a privilege.'

'What do you pray for?'

'The most obvious thing is peace. Usually you pray when you are in trouble but there is also the regular routine in the morning and evening. But usually prayer would be in a time of crisis and involve repeating the set prayers. Or at bedtime you pray for a good night's sleep, using the set prayer.

'The other things that people pray for are successful business, a good wife, a good husband, for peace constantly because there is often turmoil . . . personal peace, family peace, material things and "daily bread". You pray for exams, for a child, for somebody who is sick to get better.'

Prayer can be addressed to any god – whichever is most approachable or appropriate for the situation.

What about praying for others? Some believe there is a danger that you may be taking on their *karma,* or interfering

in the cosmic cycle of their *karma*. Others believe that when
they pray, especially when they repeat certain *mantras*, it
releases vibrations which can have powerful effects and
benefit others.

Festivals

Festivals are family and community events – perhaps the most
important form of worship for many. They are celebrated at
home and at the temples.

Diwali is the most popular. If you drive down the main
street of Leicester at *Diwali*, the shops are full of colour and
light, with crowds of people shopping, buying presents for
family and friends. In the evening the mayor comes to
inaugurate the main illuminations. At home the houses are
all lit up. Most just have electric lights but some actually use
the original oil lights that are still found in India. *Diwali*
includes a number of different themes. There is the triumph
of good over evil and light over darkness. The story of the
Ramayana – Rama's victory and safe return with Sita – is the
background. The lights celebrate the victory of good over
evil but they are also kept on to welcome Lakshmi, the
goddess of wealth, and the New Year. Even if you are away
from home, you may give instructions for all the lights to be
put on during that time, so as not to miss the opportunity.
Along with the lights go the fireworks – the louder the better
as far as the boys are concerned. Then there is food and of
course the wonderful *Diwali* sweets.

Janmashtami is the birthday of Krishna. At Bhaktivedanta
Manor, the mansion donated by George Harrison to the Hare
Krishna movement, the festival draws thousands every August.

Three weeks before *Diwali*, there is another major festival,
celebrating another victory. In most places this is the victory
of the goddess Devi over the demon Mahishasura. The
festival lasts nine or ten nights. In Gujerat it is called
Navaratri (nine nights). In Eastern India, especially Bengal, it
is *Durga Puja* (Worship of Durga – one of the names of the
Mother Goddess). She is seen astride her lion, triumphant
over the demon. In Nepal the festival is *Dasai* and includes
the sacrifice of many goats. Across North India it is called

Dussehra and has the additional focus on Rama's victory over Ravana, the nine-headed demon from Sri Lanka. In Delhi's Ram Lila Maidan, a large open field, the preparations begin some weeks ahead. Huge effigies of Ravana are made of paper and bamboo, filled with straw and fireworks. Over the nights of the festival the stories of the *Ramayana* are retold and then comes the climax, as Ravana is set on fire, with plumes of smoke, bursts of flame and the deafening noise of exploding fireworks.

Fasting

Fasting is usually individual or within the family, often linked to days of the week or the phases of the moon. It may be a total fast or restricted diet. For example, some families observe Monday, the day of Shiva, as a vegetarian day (they may not normally be strict vegetarians). Sonia fasts on Friday, in honour of Santoshi Maa. She doesn't eat during the day and at night she eats simple food, avoiding anything made from wheat. Women fast more often than men. Some do so each month, at full or new moon. They eat nothing until they sight the moon at night, when they break the fast. Apart from these regular occasions, some fast for a particular need, perhaps linked to a vow – prayer for a child, success in business, making key decisions. In some parts of North India, wives observe *Karva Chauth*, a day once a year when they fast for their husbands' health and well-being.

The *Kumbh Mela*

Hindu worship involves all the senses – light, colour, sound, movements, smells. While some pray and meditate in silence and solitude, many acts of worship are done with other people, sometimes in big crowds, at festivals or at the 'mega gatherings' called a *mela* (literally 'together'). A *mela* ranges from a village fair, complete with shrines for worship, music, food stalls and entertainment, to the vast *Kumbh Mela* which is held every three years in four North Indian cities, Allahabad, Haridwar, Ujjain, Nasik (a twelve-year cycle for each place). These places were chosen because drops of the nectar of immortality fell here from a *kumbh* – a jar which the gods were struggling to take from the demons. They regularly attract two to three million people to bathe in one of the holy rivers. The 1989 *mela* in Allahabad brought together fifteen million, the largest recorded gathering on earth.[2]

Pilgrimage

Pilgrimage is an important spiritual activity. The holy places may be temples, shrines, mountains, the source of sacred rivers, or the sea. If you visit the Marina beach at Madras you will often see busloads of pilgrims pouring out on the sand and down to the sea to dip in the waves and pray. They are usually shaven-headed, which means their tour has already taken them to the great temple at Tirupati, where worshippers offer their hair to the Lord Venkateshwara. This temple has tremendous wealth and prestige and thousands come to pray, make vows and catch a glimpse of the deity. To see, or be in the presence of a deity, a holy person, or even a sacred place, is called *darshan**. This literally means 'seeing', but it is much more. It is a moment of insight, a vision, a feeling of a presence, that stays with the worshipper.

The meaning of worship

What is the central meaning of Hindu worship? Where does it lead? We can roughly link the meaning and purpose of Hindu worship with the three major ways to salvation of the classical tradition. We referred to them in chapter 5:

- the way of knowledge – *jnana marg*.
- the way of devotion – *bhakti marg*.
- the way of action – *karma marg*.

To these we can add:

- the way of sacrifice and ritual.
- the release of power – *shakti*.

Salvation through knowledge (*jnana marg*)

The way of knowledge is linked to meditation. This in turn is linked to two basic, inter-twining ideas: the realisation that the *atman* within you is Brahman, or in other words, 'discovering the God within you'; and controlling the body and mind in order to be free from their limitations.

The mystics, from the *Upanishads* onwards, conducted experiments in consciousness. They tapped into psychic powers that enabled them to arise above normal consciousness, to travel in time and space, to see visions and have out-of-body experiences. This could lead to the trance-like experience of *samadhi* or to Shirley MacLaine's experiences, or the claims to 'yogic flying' of Maharishi Mahesh Yogi's Natural Law Party.

The Maharishi, who came to fame through the Beatles, was able to present the way of knowledge (*jnana*), in an accessible form. Transcendental Meditation is introduced through a *mantra*, a sacred phrase whispered to the initiates, who use that to focus their meditation. Ten to fifteen minutes is all you need to quieten your mind, lower your blood pressure, and reduce aggression. 'Imagine diving into the ocean . . . you consciously "dive" below deep underlying anxieties – that row with the partner or uncertainty with the boss – to settle for twenty minutes or so in the undisturbed core of your mind . . . The *mantra* on which you focus enables you to transcend thought.'[3]

Madeleine, a New Ager seeking truth, describes her experience of the way of knowledge:

'I meditated first on the flame of a candle and then into the realm of "Who am I? Who is this I that is meditating . . . ?"

'It was an intense time and through fasting and very spiritual disciplines, one day, during meditation I became what I was . . . It was as if I were staring out over the whole world, I was the grass, I was the trees, I was the people crying with hunger, I was in the sea, I was in the birds. Everything that existed, I was in all of it . . . It was a wonderful thing and I achieved it. And then I came back to this body, I, who was the God of everything. I walked down the streets, but people did not know me. And the experience became one of isolation and loneliness.'

Yoga

The way of knowledge is inextricably linked with the practice of *yoga*.

For most people outside India, the word *yoga* suggests classes where you learn to keep fit (and improve your attitude). But *yoga* means much more than that. The word is used in a number of ways. It literally means 'union', from the same root as the word 'yoke' in English. It is best described as a mental discipline through which the Self can attain union with the Absolute. These mental disciplines began to be developed even before the *Upanishads*. They were organised into the classical system by **Patanjali** (100 AD). He identified various types or stages, including physical exercise and breathing (sometimes called *hatha yoga*).

The word *yoga* is also used in some texts to describe the three paths to salvation. So you may find references to *jnana yoga, bhakti yoga, karma yoga*. In this sense the word is used for any kind of spiritual activity.

The classical sense of *yoga* is a mental and physical discipline that leads ultimately to a state of pure consciousness in *samadhi* united with the Absolute. Patanjali defines *yoga* as *citta-vritti-nirodha*, 'the suppression of the modifications of the mind'. This is reached by a series of disciplines, first to remove moral distractions (such as violence, theft, indiscipline) and then physical distractions, through correct posture (*asana**) and controlled breathing (*pranayama**). As you control your breathing, you can control your senses. And as they come to rest you can control your mental activity, concentrating more and more until you are free to exist in perfect self-consciousness.

The aim of *yoga* is to empty yourself, to close down all the openings and activities of the body until they cease to distract. So for some Hindus prayer means emptying the mind, concentrating on words, a picture, an image or beads, until the Self is merged with Brahman. It is not a personal conversation or relationship. Some do it by getting up very early in the morning or staying up late at night, when they can be quiet and undisturbed. Others use a steaming kettle and hot towel for a 'steam meditation' – up to two hours a day.

As they enter this state of emptiness, some people see bright lights or find themselves on different cosmic levels. People like Aldous Huxley, Timothy Leary, thousands of hippies, and probably many Hindu holy men, have used drugs to help them to achieve these states of altered consciousness. But orthodox Hinduism certainly does not approve of taking drugs.

Salvation through action *(karma marg)*
This is perhaps the simplest path, where a person strives to act in a way that is positive and helpful, doing good and avoiding evil. The *Bhagavad Gita* advocated the ideal of 'selfless action', without hope of reward or selfish desire. Swami Vivekananda and Mahatma Gandhi were considered ideal examples of a *karma yogi* – a person following the path of action, coming closer to God through good deeds. Mother Teresa is respected by millions of Hindus for the same reason.

In practice, the way of action means doing your duty, fulfilling your *dharma*, and so improving your *karma*.

Salvation through devotion *(bhakti marg)*
The way of devotion is often linked with singing. All the *bhakti* movements, from the sixth century onwards, expressed themselves in songs of love and devotion to a personal God. Today a group of women may gather in a home to sing *bhajans* (songs of worship). In the Southampton temple, the Sai Baba group meets each week for this. Hare Krishna worshippers may process through the streets or sit together for a night of *kirtan*. Sometimes other kinds of prayer spill over into this type:

'In our family a typical *mantra* was *Om namah Shiva*. We would sing it 108 times, over and over, till the people got into a frenzy and started dancing. It was almost as though they were possessed. The music was going on and there was constant singing and banging of bells, and everybody was in a frenzy. At the end it was almost like a climax and you have been on some kind of journey. There is no doubt that you feel different at the end of it – maybe a form of spiritual exercise.'

Dance is an important way of expressing devotion in worship. In South India the classical Bharata Natyam was connected with the worship of Shiva. In Orissa the Odissi dance form was devoted to Krishna. Neera Kapur describes its background:

'My dance goes back to the twelfth century, based on the Gita Govinda. In these poems the devotee is Radha and the god is Krishna. When they unite, the two of them become one and that is like a sensual relationship with God. You are one with God straightaway. You don't need Sanskrit texts. You have your songs and that is enough. It's a way of direct access by an emotional experience.'

This kind of dance expresses devotion but also union. 'It's like the individual spirit becoming fused with the universal spirit.' In her case the dance has gone beyond *bhakti* to an expression of cosmic unity: 'In my dance I feel like a small particle floating in the cosmic all. The whole universe is the dance of Shiva, the cosmic energy.'

In the Sai Baba communities in England, they use keyboard music to help their worship. 'You don't have to give up your cultural identity to follow the guru,' explains the leader.

For most *bhakti* worshippers, whether through song, dance or spoken prayer, their devotion remains linked to a personal God. They feel a sense of unworthiness and longing for God: they seek union but not total absorption.

Salvation through sacrifice and ritual

In a smart Delhi suburb it is a crisp, sunny Monday morning. Five people gather around a fireplace built into Dr Mehta's lawn. There are logs burning in the fireplace. An elderly man fans the logs while Dr Mehta chants Sanskrit *slokas** and puts *ghee* (clarified butter) on the fire. At the end of each chant the others join in the closing word: '*Swahaah* . . .' and throw grain or fruits or sweets on the fire from the metal trays which they are holding. The *mantras* which he is chanting are addressed to different gods – Shiva, Bhairava (a lieutenant of Shiva), Hanuman, Ram (a lieutenant of Vishnu), Suriya (the sun), Isa Masih (Jesus Christ).

'This Gayatri Mantra is very powerful,' comments Dr

Mehta. 'It can raise the dead if you chant it 125,000 times. Today we are praying for all sick people in general. Our prayers are releasing vibrations and an aura which cleanses the atmosphere.'

The ceremonies come to a close with the offering of *arti*. Each person waves the lamp in turn, reciting a prayer. Finally all bow in the direction of the guru whose picture stands at one side – Hirakhand Baba from Almora.

This is a *havan**, a fire sacrifice. A *havan* can be performed on any special occasion, like the opening of a new building or preparation for a marriage. This group does it regularly every Monday morning. It is a ritual which goes back to the old period of the Vedas but has largely been replaced by *puja*, the worship of the images.

The practice of sacrifice has largely disappeared, except in the *havan* and the occasional practice of animal sacrifice, for example in the Kali temple in Calcutta, or at the Dasai festival in Nepal. But the ideas which lay behind the old sacrifices still remain in much ritual and prayer today.

A *mantra* is really a spell, a sound that has power, that releases vibrations and an aura. *OM* is the ultimate *mantra*, the most important sound, expressing the power that created the universe.

It is important to get the ritual right, to achieve the desired results. So the priest has a key role and what he says and does is important, even if the others do not fully understand it: 'A mantra chanted with mistakes in it is worse than chanting no mantra at all. Personally I feel that like all other mantras this [*Gayatri*] mantra is of Tantric origin and that may be why it has locked within itself unexplainable powers.'[4]

Some forms of asceticism or prayer are linked with the ancient idea of *tapas** (literally heat). In many of the old stories a person performs some extraordinary action of devotion or asceticism which generates *tapas*. Eventually this has such power that the gods are forced to answer the request which the person is making. There is perhaps a link here with the ancient religions of the Middle East (Mesopotamia and Canaan), which sometimes put the gods under pressure to fulfil their functions. Mahatma Gandhi's fasts were a kind of *tapas*, creating moral pressure which other people could not resist.

Salvation through the release of power (*shakti*)

A distinct stream in the Hindu tradition is linked with worship of the Mother Goddess, the feminine principle or *shakti*. In this tradition there are certain practices through which the power can be released.

These principles are sometimes referred to as *tantra*. This word is used in a variety of ways. In a general sense it refers to any practice that does not come from the *Vedas*. More specifically it refers to those practices that seek to activate and release divine powers within a person through certain rituals. Some tantric practices are linked with meditation, recitation or focusing on an image, through which the worshipper can be identified with that image's powers. Others seek to release a person's inner creative powers by using them in rituals, including forbidden practices like eating meat, drinking wine and sexual intercourse. This type of ritual, known as the 'left handed' *tantra*, is practised by a minority. But the search for power, and the belief that it can be released in a person, is very widespread.

The *tantra* tradition has also developed a special kind of *yoga* discipline known as *kundalini**, the serpent power coiled up at the base of the spine. Through exercises and controlled breathing, this power can be released: 'When it uncoils and starts rising, it progressively penetrates seven *chakras* or centres along the spinal system until it finally bursts in ecstasy into the thousand-petalled lotus in the cerebral cortex and the yogi is flooded with . . . contact with the Brahman.'[5]

Karan Singh goes on to compare this experience with the effects of certain drugs like LSD, which has 'opened the minds of many in the West who previously had decisively dismissed the whole *kundalini* phenomenon'.[6] However, he does not advocate drug taking as the right way to higher consciousness.

Which way is best?
The only answer is: choose what is best for you. In the *Bhagavad Gita* Krishna expressly said that all ways are equally valid. In fact, he says, all of them are summed up in worship and devotion to him: 'He who offers me with devotion a leaf, a flower, fruit or water, that devout offering of a pure minded one I accept.'[7]

In practice, people combine different ways, consciously or subconsciously mixing and matching what suits them best.

Whatever way you choose, a *guru* is indispensable. A guru can explain things clearly and prescribe the beliefs and practices that are best for you. Finding the right guru whom you can trust, and following the path that the guru sets for you, could be your most important step on the path to God.

Reflection
Hindu worship involves discipline and devotion. It is rich in ritual and appeals to all the senses with its light, colour, sound, music and smells.

It is very diverse and leads in different directions. The classical ways to salvation actually represent quite different ideas. Is the aim complete nothingness (*yoga*)? Is it an experience of unity with the Absolute and the whole universe (Madeleine's story)? Is it emotional experience (*bhakti*)? Or release of power (*shakti*)? Or does it lead to a relationship between God and the worshipper?

Some would answer that these are all valid goals. It would depend on the individual and the stage they have reached.

These different ways have many similarities to Christian worship, with one radical qualification, which we explore in chapter 10 (page 159). For Christians the focus of all worship is God, who has become known to us through Jesus Christ. So all their devotion and actions of service and love are offered through him, in his name. He is also the one who inspires them to express their gratitude, love, adoration, prayer for forgiveness and prayer for others.

1. The *Gayatri Mantra*, a prayer to the Creator and to the Sun (from the *Rig Veda* 3.62.10), prayed by millions of Hindus at sunrise and many other times. The Sanskrit words are in-

terpreted differently by different people. The rendering here is taken from the Vedic Temple in Southampton.

2. *Guinness Book of Records*.
3. *Telegraph Magazine*, March 1996.
4. Ed Viswanathan, *Am I a Hindu? The Hinduism Primer* (Rupa and Co., Calcutta, 1993), p. 163.
5. Karan Singh, *Essays on Hinduism* (Ratna Sagar, Delhi, 1990), p. 90.
6. ibid., p. 91.
7. *Bhagavad Gita* 9.26.

7

Ethics and Morality

The true Vaishnava is the one who feels another's
  sufferings as his own.
Even if he helps the sufferer, he doesn't feel proud.
He looks on everything dispassionately, he has abandoned
  desire, another's wife is like his mother.
He is without greed and bereft of deceit, he has turned
  away from lust and anger.
Narasaimyo says at the sight of him, the family is saved for
  seventy-one generations.[1]

Why are Asian corner shops successful? Do they just work harder? Or is it their strong sense of family loyalty? Is it the drive to make money, or a more competitive spirit?

Unfortunately we can't pursue these interesting questions here. But even corner shops face ethical questions, like conflicts of duty. When the head of a family of newsagents died, the family were expected to follow custom by closing their shops for three days, to fulfil the rituals and as a mark of respect. Their competitors gladly offered to help by supplying their customers! But the family decided not to close – and argued that this was what their father would have expected. Which way did their real duty lie?

One of the most famous case studies in ethics is another conflict of duty. It's the story of Krishna and Arjuna, just before the great battle of Kurukshetra.

Arjuna is facing a moral crisis. As he prepares for battle he can see his close relatives, his respected teachers, on the opposing side. It is his duty to kill them – but how can he do it?

Krishna, his charioteer, explains that he is facing a conflict of duty. On one side is his duty to love and respect his relatives and teachers. On the other is the higher obligation to fulfil his *dharma* as a warrior. He also reminds Arjuna that death is not the end; it is a stage to the next life in the cycle of birth and rebirth.

Most Hindus learn morality through stories – the stories which they have heard from childhood, like the story of Krishna and Arjuna. The epics and the *Puranas* contain many other stories about gods, wise people, kings, princes and ordinary people, which all provide examples of how to behave in different situations. Rama, the hero of the *Ramayana*, is the ideal king and husband, the outstanding example, whom we can and should copy. 'Lord Krishna is beyond us to follow, but it *is* possible for us to be like Lord Rama,' is a common view.

Fundamental principles: dharma *and* karma

Krishna's answers to Arjuna are based on the two fundamental principles behind Hindu ideas of morality:

- *dharma* – the unique duty that each person must fulfil
- *karma* – the law of cause and effect which determines the outcome of all our actions

The important thing for Arjuna is that he fulfils his *dharma*, when he follows Krishna's advice. So does Rama, even though it is costly. Fulfilling your *dharma* is the essence of morality.

What is your *dharma*? There is no absolute answer, because it depends who and where you are. In the classical tradition, *dharma* is community based, rather than individual. It is summed up in *varnashrama dharma*, the system established by the priests, based on *varna* (caste) and *ashrama** (stages of life). Each group and sub-group within the caste system had its own *dharma*, which applied to all the members of that group. It was set out in codes like the *Laws of Manu*, while the Epics and *Puranas* showed how these ideals were lived out by the heroes of the past.

Dharma is based on relationships

Dharma is based first of all on relationships within the community. You are born into your extended family and your caste. So you are a part of a network of relationships, with automatic responsibilities and duties. For example, as an older brother you are responsible (under your father and uncles) for the welfare of your younger brothers and the care and protection of your sisters. In return, you receive their affection, dependence and obedience. When a girl 'gets into trouble' with a young man, whether in an Indian village or a Chicago suburb, her brothers are expected to look after her, bring her back and deal with the offending youth. The festival of *rakshabandhan* in August expresses the close relationship between brothers and sisters. Girls tie a *rakhi*, a brightly coloured string, on their brother's wrist, or the wrist of another male relative or close friend. It's not a symbol of romance but of sisterly affection and of coming under his protection.

Hindu family life – like all South Asian family life – is full of warmth and affection. Children are brought up in close relationships with their cousins (thought of as brothers and sisters), and with uncles, aunts and grandparents. Adult friends of the family are automatically 'uncle' and 'auntie'. Family honour and prestige *(izzat*)* is more important than individual fulfilment. Rama was willing to go into exile for fourteen years to uphold his father's (unwise) promise. Later, he sacrificed his wife Sita for the sake of family honour. An individual's actions reflect credit – or shame – on the whole family. Young people have this drummed into them: 'If you've got a screwed up *izzat* [family reputation], nobody wants to know you. And how will your sisters get good husbands if you behave like this?'

Dharma is based on the stages and goals of life

In the classical tradition, there were **four stages** of life (*ashramas*) for a Hindu man:

- *brahmacharya** – the pupil stage of knowledge and wisdom: the boy was initiated through the sacred thread

ceremony and studied the *Vedas* under a teacher or a priest.
This stage was open to all in theory, but in practice
was only an option for the higher castes and privileged
groups.

● *gryhasta** – the married householder, building up one's
fortunes: the most significant stage. The duty to marry,
continue the family and care for it, was a social and
religious requirement.

● *vanaprastha** – retirement from the world and beginning
to secure one's spiritual welfare: literally 'going into the
forest' to live as a hermit, meditating on the scriptures. In
practice it was the stage of handing over responsibility to
the oldest son, when the father became a grandfather.

● *sannyas** – complete renunciation of the world, preparing
for the ultimate detachment of *moksha*: an optional stage,
perhaps an indication that a person was near the end of
the cycle of rebirths.

Along with these there were **four goals** in life

● *Kama** – fulfilling bodily desires.
● *Artha** – economic and political activity.
● *Dharma* – behaving rightly, fulfilling one's duty.
● *Moksha* – release from this life.

Each goal is legitimate, as long as it is fulfilled in a way that
does not clash with higher goals. Above the first three – to
some extent in tension with them – is the ultimate goal of
moksha.

The four stages were always an ideal rather than rigidly
enforced. Today they are seen as a reminder of the balance
between fulfilling earthly responsibilities (especially for the
family) and preparing for the inner life, or the next life. The
vast majority of Hindu men, if they think about it consciously,
see themselves as fulfilling their duty as family members and
householders. A smaller number move to the stage of activat-
ing their spiritual life, while a very small minority are called
to the life of renunciation and spiritual enlightenment.

In the same way the four goals give balance in life and

ensure the continuance of a stable society.

Dharma is based on community and caste

This community-based *dharma* aims at a society in which each group follows its own unique way, not interfering with the privileges and responsibilities of other groups. And within this each individual fulfils their unique role, according to their community and stage in life.

There can never be absolutes in this system. The only 'absolute' is to do your own duty, whatever that may be. Behind and above all that you do is the law of *karma*, which also helps to define your duty. Your present situation is the result of past *karma*, and your future situation depends on what you do now.

The caste system, which is the basis of this *dharma*, has given considerable stability to society. There is a strong sense of mutual responsibility and care. One reason why Asian businesses flourish is because the family members all share in the work. (This is true not only for Hindus but for Asians of any religious background.) The extended family can provide credit or capital for new business, if needed. Caste associations operate like trade guilds, to help their members.

But responsibility is often limited to one's own community. In general, people are not expected to care for those of other caste groups. The system works well when each group looks after itself and doesn't interfere with others. Then there can be peaceful co-existence and interdependence. In practice, there are tensions between caste groups. We shall look at these, and the ethics of caste, in chapter 8.

Getting behind dharma

Can we go a bit deeper to see how the average person views *dharma*? Here are some questions they might ask.

What is the point of being good?

What is the motivation for ethical behaviour? For some it is the hope of *moksha* (liberation). Following *dharma* leads to 'the attainment of perfection, self realisation and God realisation. It brings about happiness, speedy spiritual evolution and freedom (*moksha*). One attains immortality, perennial bliss, freedom from the yoke of *maya* and a place in the service of the Lord in His highest abode.'[2]

Moksha is the most important goal. But it could lead you to conclude that the other goals are unimportant. You could lose any motivation to change unsatisfactory conditions in this life. In practice, not many consider themselves ready to expect *moksha*. Their duty is still to concentrate on the earlier stages and goals.

In the *advaita* system where the ultimate deity is impersonal, the Absolute Brahman is actually beyond good and evil. So morality is important at a lower stage, but the highest stage is knowledge and spiritual insight. The *jivanmukta*, who has reached that stage (chapter 5), is beyond good and evil.

Those who follow several gods could be tempted to lower their standards: if one demands too much, you could try another. And you may not always be sure what a particular deity does want.

For some the concept of *karma* is a motivation for doing good. But it could also lead to complacency. In a BBC travel programme, Clive Anderson was struck by the extremes of wealth and poverty in Calcutta. 'Don't you find this a problem?' he asked a well-to-do woman at a reception. 'You see,' she replied, 'we believe in *karma* – each person's fate is determined by their own actions . . .' So there is nothing you can do to change their situation. On the other hand, you could gain some merit by helping others – but not necessarily in this life.

Many recognise this dilemma but affirm that the concept of *karma* is not meant to lead you to indifference to others.

In the *bhakti* tradition, fulfilling *dharma* can be an offering to the Lord, which is pleasing to him. Or the guru may provide the inspiration, as Swami Bhakti Vallabh of the Swaminarayan Mission in Neasden explains: 'We want to serve God and our guru because our guru loves us so much.'

What about ritual?

Dharma and *karma* are impersonal principles which operate independently of the gods. The gods themselves are under the control of *karma*. *Dharma* is linked to *rta*, the ordering principle of the universe. So as individuals fulfil their *dharma*, they are helping to maintain the cosmic order. Sacrifices and ritual are crucial for this. And so ritual purity and pollution have been as important, if not more important, than moral or immoral actions. At the beginning of the nineteenth century, reformers like Ram Mohun Roy found that breaking dietary laws brought much worse penalties than stealing or murder. There were elaborate regulations for maintaining purity, particularly in relation to diet, personal hygiene and avoiding being touched by somebody of a different (lower) caste. In some Hindu homes today the kitchen is seen as a centre of purity. People remove their shoes and in some cases bathe before entering it.

Some of these regulations were similar to the ritual laws of the people of Israel, described in the Hebrew scriptures accepted by Jews, Christians and Muslims. They had been multiplied by the religious leaders by the time of Jesus in the New Testament.[3] He went behind them to the inner attitudes.

What does it mean to be good?

The last few paragraphs may be a bit abstract for the average person, who knows that it is right to be good and do one's duty. But what does it mean to be good? Here are some people's suggestions:

'Be kind, don't tell lies, tell what is in your heart. Don't speak evil about others. Don't be selfish.'

'Be helpful, sober, co-operative.'

'Don't backbite.'

'We should live for others, not for ourselves. The one who lives for self is not a great personality.'

How do you know what is right?

'If your heart agrees, it is right. After you have prayed, if your heart is clean, *apne aap bataega* (it will tell you itself).'

This was also Mahatma Gandhi's view: he always listened to his 'inner voice' to tell him what he should do.

'A good person will have a shine on his face.' So prayer and reflection are important in helping to decide what is right. Ultimately, you must decide for yourself. But also: 'We learn from examples of the past, especially Lord Rama.' 'It is good to follow the teaching of gurus.'

Some teachers have given clear instructions to their followers. The Swaminarayan Mission, for example, has the *Shikshapatri* ('letter of instruction'), 212 verses of essential spiritual and ethical teaching. The original Sanskrit collection has been edited into a small booklet, in Gujerati and English, which each devotee is expected to read each day. Topics include:

- Code for an ethical life – 'do not gamble, do not steal; not even for a religious or a benevolent cause.'
- Non-violence – 'do not kill any living creature.'
- On being practical in life – 'maintain a daily account of income and expenditure. Do not indulge in any extravagant expenses.'
- Code for food, drink and ecology – 'do not consume tobacco, hemp, hashish and such intoxicants. Do not eat non-vegetarian food containing eggs, fish or animal flesh.'
- Code for sane sex conduct – 'do not commit adultery. Do not wear clothes that are exhibitive, exciting or bewitching to the opposite sex. O married men and women, be loving, loyal and faithful to one another. Do not be harsh to one another.'

The practical down-to-earth rules are reminiscent of the salty common sense of the book of Proverbs in the Old Testament. Similar books of proverbs and moral advice can be found in other Indian cultures, such as the *Thirukural*, written in Tamil by a wise man Thiruvalluvar about the first century AD. Every bus in Madras carries quotations from it.

Other important ethical ideas

Ahimsa

A key concept, which goes back as far as the *Upanishads*, is *ahimsa*, non-violence. The older texts did not particularly emphasise it, but it became an important principle of the early Buddhists and even more of the Jains. The great emperor Ashoka, who became a Buddhist, was convicted of the importance of *ahimsa*. He gave up war and became a vegetarian.

Vegetarianism

Through Buddhist and Jain influence, animal sacrifices were mostly replaced by offerings of grain, flowers, fruits (especially coconuts), milk and *ghee* (clarified butter). Vegetarianism became a major part of Hindu belief and practice. This is probably the most enduring aspect of *ahimsa*. Interestingly, it was not a total ban on non-vegetarian food. The *Laws of Manu* commented: 'Meat eating is not wrong, nor alcohol, nor sex. These are natural actions of living beings; but abstention from such action is highly rewarded.'[4]

The Jains were the strictest in their concern to avoid violence to any living being. They gave up agriculture because of the destruction of creatures in the soil. Most Jains moved into business, where they became extremely successful. Jain traders from Gujerat and Rajasthan (*Marwaris*) have spread all over India and more recently around the world. Orthodox Jains do not eat food after dark, in case they accidentally swallow an insect. Jain monks wear a white mask over their nose and mouth to avoid breathing in some tiny creature.

For some, protecting the cow is an important symbol of Hindu ethical values. Groups like the Vishwa Hindu Parishad mount periodic campaigns for a total ban on cow slaughter throughout India (sometimes more for political than religious reasons). The recent crisis over beef in the UK and the subsequent slaughter of cattle caused distress to many Hindus.

For many, vegetarianism is linked with reincarnation and the belief that all living beings are of equal value: 'On a Brahmin full of knowledge and good conduct, on a cow, or on an elephant, on a dog, or on a person of unclean caste, wise men look with equal eye.'[5]

The *Gita*: action without attachment

As we saw earlier, there is a major tension in Hindu ethics between the ideal of *detachment* from this life, which is ultimately unreal, and *commitment* to action, in order to fulfil one's duty. The *Bhagavad Gita* introduced an important concept to resolve the tension – action without desire or attachment, *nishkama karma*. Actions appear to keep us tied to the wheel of *sansara* – continued existence in the cycle of birth and re-birth. But, Krishna points out, it is not the action but the attitude behind the action. If we can make our actions an offering to the divine, if we can remain untroubled by their consequences (good or bad) then they can help our spiritual development, not hinder it.

Chandu Malkani, a London businessman and student of the *Gita*, quotes Sadhu Vaswani who explained this as 'find freedom *in* action, not *from* action' or (quoting Jesus) 'be *in* the world but not *of* the world'. It is like parents who are not hurt if their child does not appreciate their care. Or those who give selfless service without thinking of reward or recognition. This is the difference, he says, between politicians and truly great people.

On this view, attachment to the world of appearance, or emphasis on the *ego*, are the enemies. We must kill our attachment to the things of the body.

Where does evil come from?

This raises the question: what is the basic source of evil? What is understood by wrong or sin? For some Hindus, the basic problem of life, the source of evil, is *not* primarily moral. It is not seen as sin or disobedience or rebellion against God. It is rather our ignorance of the true nature of things. Many regard the material world as the source of our problems:

Maya means *prakriti* [*primary matter*].
It is the basic substance and the cause of all bondage.
Its nature is of darkness and ignorance.

Its constituents are the three *gunas*, namely, *sattva*, *rajas* and
    tamas.
It is the cause of ego and attachment to the body and its
    relations.[6]

Darkness and ignorance are therefore a part of the material
world. Our entanglement with this drags us down. But if we
realise this, we can become free. The solution is knowledge.
'Ignorance is the root of all evil. Knowledge eradicates ignorance. That is the way the idea of sin is explained in Hinduism.'[7]

Food
Some extend this to what you eat. Food can be ritually
polluting, if it comes from a person of a lower caste. The
qualities of the person who cooked the food, or handled it,
enter into it. In addition, foods have an inherent quality –
one of the three *gunas* (chapter 5). Some food has the quality
of *tamas* (e.g. meat, alcohol). It conveys inertia and dullness.
Some has the quality of *rajas* (e.g. spicy or salty food, chilli).
It stimulates excitement and action. Other food has the
quality of *sattva*: it promotes health and intelligence (e.g.
grains, vegetables, milk products). You become what you eat
– not just your physical health but your character. ISKCON
members are very careful about their diet for this reason.

The reform movements
By the end of the eighteenth century Hindu society had become
inward-looking and controlled by superstition (chapter 2).
The renaissance movements of the nineteenth and early
twentieth centuries focused on social reform. Many were
explicitly influenced by Christian or liberal European values.
Some reacted against them, like the Arya Samaj, while others
consciously absorbed what they felt was good into their own
system.

A wider concern
Apart from getting rid of superstitious practices, the reformers' main thrust was to find a new basis for *dharma* that
went beyond the narrow limits of one's own caste and

community. For many this was a radical change.

Ram Mohun Roy worked with the Christian missionary William Carey and his colleagues to campaign against *sati* (widow-burning). Swami Vivekananda advocated 'practical *vedanta*'. This includes 'work without attachment' which helps a person to realise the truth. Then the person who has reached the 'threshold of final liberation' willingly steps back into the world to serve others. Vivekananda combined a strong emphasis on *vedanta* and knowledge with practical social reform.

Mahatma Gandhi developed a unique blend of values from Hindu and other sources, such as the Sermon on the Mount and Tolstoy, as we saw in chapter 2. He started from *satya* (truth) and *ahimsa* (non-violence). But he transformed them. *Ahimsa* became 'passive resistance to evil, wherever it is found', through 'truth force' (*satyagraha*). This immediately widened the basis for concern – it was anybody in need, whether untouchables, Muslims or high caste Hindus. And *ahimsa* meant resisting evil through suffering for others, or in other words, through love.

Gandhi also emphasised the concept of *sarvodaya**, the good of the whole community, based on his reading of John Ruskin's book *Unto this Last*. 'The good of the individual is contained in the good of all.' He believed that the best way to implement this was at the village level, where a community could be self-sufficient. He had a vision of India as a network of self-sufficient village communities. He called his *ashram** community at Wardha '*Sevagram*' (village of service).

Today Gandhi's ideals are respected but not practised. The vision of the village has been replaced by urbanisation and industrialisation. Passive resistance could not last beyond the Chinese invasion of 1962, the constant tensions with Pakistan, or the nuclear threat. And truth and the common welfare have been the casualties of increasing corruption and materialism.

Some issues today

Hindus today, like everybody else, face a range of pressing ethical issues.

Family matters

Family life is under pressure from urbanisation, which makes it much harder for extended families to live together. Elderly parents and relatives have always been cared for in the family and this is still the norm. But urban pressure means that a small but growing number are cared for in homes for the elderly. While some accept this, it is a shock for others. Divorce is permitted but there are strong family pressures against it, especially if the woman takes the initiative.

The main purpose of sexual activity has traditionally been the procreation of children. Abstaining from sex was considered to increase a person's physical and spiritual strength. Artificial methods of birth control have been opposed by some, but population pressures and government campaigns have resulted in widespread acceptance of contraceptives. Abortion is traditionally considered a great sin, as life begins at conception, but it has become common and is almost a method of birth control for some. The modern technique of amniocentesis can determine the sex of the unborn child, which has resulted in the abortion of female infants (made illegal in India in 1994).

Daughters are still considered less valuable than sons and the practice of dowry (paid by the bride's parents) continues. This can place great pressure on the girl's family. In some cases it is so extreme that the girl is forced into suicide, or even murdered by her in-laws. In a city like Delhi there are still several hundred cases of 'accidental' deaths of young wives each year.

India may become the epicentre of the AIDS crisis of the twenty-first century. There are reckoned to be 1.75 million people who are HIV positive, rising to four million by the year 2000. The infection is being spread primarily through heterosexual contact with prostitutes in the major urban centres. Disturbingly, there is an increasing number of 'respectable' middle-class professional families among those being infected. Drug abuse, mostly in the North East region, is the second major cause, followed by contaminated blood in hospital blood transfusions. The official response so far focuses mostly on techniques for safer sex, rather than any overt reference to religious or moral factors.[8]

Environment

The Hindu view of the environment is based on the inter-connectedness of all living things. Animals, trees, rivers and mountains have always been considered with reverence and there are many stories of people who protected animals in the past. Of course, this does not always translate into practical concern today. People can worship nature but do nothing to sustain it. And this view is held in increasing tension with economic and technological imperatives which lead to great pressure on the environment. In India, Nehru's commitment to heavy industry brought factories, power plants and massive dams, with all their implications, good and bad.

There is also the tension between the goal of *artha*, which seeks profit, and *dharma*, which upholds righteousness. The pressure is much greater in developing countries where protecting the environment is expensive and resources are scarce. South Asian countries face problems of deforestation, which leads to soil erosion and flooding, and of industrial pollution, urban slums and waste disposal. Ranchor Prime describes the neglect of the environment in Vrindavan, Krishna's birthplace, through factors like these.[9] The Bhopal gas tragedy in 1984, the plague scare in Surat in 1995, and epidemics of malaria and dengue in Delhi in 1996 were stark reminders of these acute pressures.

There is another tension between the ideal of hard work – held by many Hindu communities, especially farmers and business people – and the ideal of renunciation, which questions the ultimate value of work and improving the environment. Superstitions and traditional practices can also cause difficulties. Some villagers believe that certain days are inauspicious for starting new activity, so they delay planting or weeding. Caste divisions can prevent communities from working together on essential projects like tree planting or irrigation channels, which benefit them all. Some see the 'common good' as the good of their own community, regardless of others. Ecological pressures are increased by negligence, for example when people fail to dig out silted river channels, which results in damaging floods each monsoon season. They may also be increased by corruption, when government officials or contractors pocket the funds intended for tree-planting or use sub-standard material for a bridge which collapses.

Of course, these issues are not unique to South Asia. Our concern here is to try and analyse a specifically Hindu response.

One suggestion is to go back to the Gandhian ideal of village self-sufficiency. Groups like Intermediate Technology, inspired by E. F. Schumacher's *Small is Beautiful,* have come to the same conclusion from different religious backgrounds. Undoubtedly, local action and community development are effective. But it takes real commitment, especially when the gulf between city and village life is widening. Voluntary projects in India have been specially effective. Some are Hindu, some are led by people of other faiths, or from various backgrounds.

The Chipko movement in the 1970s was a dramatic protest against environmental destruction. In the foothills of the Himalayas, forests were being cut down by commercial logging companies. Women tied themselves to trees to protect them from the chain saws. They took their inspiration from village women in Rajasthan who died to protect trees in 1730. The movement was based on Gandhian non-violent resistance. Sunderlal Bahuguna, one of the leaders, based his approach on the *Bhagavad Gita*'s concept of action without attachment.

Paradoxically, in the same region, in both India and Nepal, villagers also cut off branches and leaves for fuel, destroying the trees and creating a worse energy crisis.

The global challenge
In India corruption used to be the big ethical issue – or rather non-issue, as nobody seemed able to do more than shrug their shoulders. *Chalta hai* was the expression – 'that's how it is'. At the same time, sexual morality was strictly controlled and the West was seen as degenerate, because of its permissiveness. Today corruption seems to be increasing world-wide, while

standards of sexual morality are changing in India, as films, music and satellite TV exert their relentless influence. The pressure to find a basis for maintaining ethical standards is universal. Hindus living in the West are caught in the middle.

Reflection

Hindu ethics are based on the twin principles of *dharma* and *karma*, which underlie the pattern of the universe. Some Hindus are motivated by the desire to please God or their guru. For others it is more of an attempt to conform to these impersonal and inescapable principles, through rituals as well as behaviour. Evil, as we saw, is essentially a feature of this material world, rather than a matter of moral choices. But in practice the great majority have a clear sense of right and wrong. This is based on the familiar stories of the past, which provide models of good and bad behaviour, examples of those who fulfilled their *dharma*. *Dharma* is fulfilled in relationships, largely within the family and community. So there is a continuing tension between this strong commitment to one's own group and the need to find a wider basis for care, that extends to people of other backgrounds as well. We shall explore this tension further in chapter 8.

1. From a song by Narsimha Mehta (1414–80), Gujerat's greatest poet, in the *bhakti* tradition. This song was a favourite of Mahatma Gandhi, expressing high ethical ideals.
2. Ramesh Darve, *Gems from the Shikshapatri* (Swaminarayan Mission, Ahmedabad, 1995).
3. Gospel of Mark 7:3–23.
4. The *Laws of Manu* 5.56.
5. *Bhagavad Gita* 5.18.
6. *Shikshapatri of Swaminarayan*.
7. Ed Viswanathan, *Am I a Hindu? The Hinduism Primer* (Rupa and Co., Calcutta, 1993), p. 287.
8. 'AIDS Striking Home', *India Today*, 15 March 1997.
9. Ranchor Prime, *Hinduism and Ecology: Seeds of Truth* (Cassell, 1992), p. 108.

8

Religious Structures

The priest is the Lord of this whole creation.[1]

*The ascetic should live here on earth in ecstatic
    contemplation of the soul,*
indifferent, without any carnal desires.[2]

Kaun batave baat guru bina,
Kaun batave baat?
*Who will explain without a guru, who will explain the
    matter?*[3]

What holds Hinduism together? Who are the accepted leaders?
Where does authority lie for Hindus?

There could be several answers to these questions. The
most obvious is that authority lies in the ancient **scriptures**
called the *Vedas* and the **priests** appointed to maintain the
ritual and social order prescribed by those scriptures.

The priests
The 1910 Census Commission of India defined Hindus as
those who accepted the authority of the Brahmin priests and
the *Vedas*.[4] Large parts of the *Vedas* consist of instructions to
the priests on the right way to conduct the rituals and sacrifices
which maintain the universe and regulate human lives. The
priests were the people who knew how to do these things
properly. They also had the authority to explain the scriptures
and guide people in the right way to live. Through the centuries
the priests have continued to have a dominant role.

Priests have traditionally been drawn from the Brahmin caste, though people of other castes serve as priests for certain communities. A recent court ruling in South India said that the appointment of priests even in temples should not be based on caste considerations.[5] Of course not all Brahmins are recognised or trained to become priests. The majority are in other professions. Becoming a priest requires years spent learning the scriptures and the rituals in Sanskrit. Traditional learning included grammar, interpretation, pronunciation, correct procedures for the rituals, and astrology. The young person learned by listening to the older priests and watching them perform their duties.

The priests play a key role at all the important stages of life – birth, growing up, weddings, new home, new buildings and finally death.

It's the night before the eldest son of the family is to get married. The extended family, with a few close friends and neighbours, get together for a preparatory ceremony. The priest sits in the centre of the room and begins to recite from the scriptures, while the others look on. The atmosphere is informal. People are in a good mood, as they should be before a wedding. They don't appear to pay very close attention to the words and actions, but it is important that they are done, and done correctly. Tomorrow there will be much more elaborate rituals in the actual wedding ceremony.

Apart from conducting rituals, priests are expected to give answers to people's questions. For example, when a person dies, the relatives are naturally very interested in exactly where the soul has gone and where it is going to be re-incarnated, which may lead on to questions about when life begins and when a new baby or unborn foetus gets its soul.

There is no centralised priesthood. Some priests are attached to temples where their main duty is to regulate the *puja* and the offerings of the worshippers. Some work part time, carrying on another profession, while available to conduct rituals for families as needed. Part of a priest's training is in astrology and for some this is their full-time occupation. In village life the priests may also have an important role as storytellers.

A priest may be called a *pandit* (referring to his teaching role), *purohit* (a family priest), or *pujari* (referring to his role as one who offers *puja*). He may be addressed by names like *panditji*, *maharaji* or *swamiji* (*ji* is a polite addition to anybody's name).

Different groups

All orthodox Hindus accept the authority of the Brahmin priests and the social hierarchy linked with it. But this leaves plenty of room for variety in belief and practice, according to people's inclination and abilities. So there are many different groups within Hinduism. Some are very broad, like the division between those who worship Vishnu (*Vaishnavites*) and those who give allegiance to Shiva (*Shaivites*). There are numerous smaller groupings, for example the Lingayats of Karnataka, a distinctive group among those who worship Shiva. There are various *bhakti* movements and *tantric* groups. Many groups arose out of reform movements of the nineteenth century, such as the Arya Samaj or the Ramakrishna Mission. 'My father was a Sanatana Dharmi, while my mother was an Arya Samaji, who don't worship idols,' says an East African woman. 'So in our home we had rituals but not much of the stories that go with them.'

The ascetics

Another source of authority in Hinduism is the broad spectrum of five to fifteen million 'holy men' (and some holy women), otherwise known as *sadhus* or 'ascetics'.

The *sadhus* have taken vows of *sannyas* or renunciation. They have chosen to withdraw from the world and follow a path of physical and mental discipline in their search for liberation. Many belong to an order and live in communities called *ashrams* – literally places of 'no labour' – where they meditate under spiritual leaders. Others wander independently or live in complete solitude. Some practise a fearsome ascetic discipline.

One of the oldest monastic orders goes right back to the great philosopher Sankara, who founded four monasteries in four corners of India to continue his teaching and ensure orthodoxy. They continue today, each led by a *Sankaracharya* ('Sankara scholar leader'). They have considerable spiritual authority and are often consulted by political leaders on issues that concern Hinduism as a whole. In 1987 the whole of India was convulsed over the Roop Kanwar case, when a young woman in Rajasthan died on her husband's funeral pyre and became a *sati* (chapter 7). One of the *Sankaracharyas* enraged popular opinion when he pronounced in favour of *sati*.

Sadhus form a kind of spiritual brotherhood or sisterhood (female *sadhus* are known as *sadhvis*). Caste plays no part in becoming a *sadhu*, so this offers release from the restrictions of social order, as well as from the cares of contemporary life. There is an initiation ceremony, which usually includes shaving the head and receiving a *mantra* and a new name. Most *sadhus* wear saffron robes and are expected to live a life of simplicity. Many are constantly on the move, usually travelling on foot (or by train, where they are entitled to free travel). The sight of a wandering holy man, with shaved head or matted hair, begging bowl and staff, is very common in India. They are expected to live on the food and offerings provided by devout Hindus. The majority are genuine but (as everywhere) some are fake and exploit people's piety for money, sexual favours, or sometimes political influence.

The most dramatic appearance of the *sadhus* is at the mammoth *Kumbh Mela* (chapter 6), where they come in their thousands to give a spiritual lead to the millions of pilgrims.

> The festival sees the massing of a great army of priests and holy men of all kinds. Here they enjoy the respect of the crowds and debate religion and philosophy. Some are carried on decorated chariots, shaded by parasols, fanned by admirers, garlands of marigolds about their necks. The most remarkable are the naked or near naked *sadhus*, their bodies smeared with ash, their hair roughly braided. They have a place in Hindu society as men truly liberated – free from work, from coercion, from obligations, from clothes. Many live by begging food and shelter; they are never

refused. Many Hindus believe that to catch sight of a naked *sadhu* removes sin.[6]

Within the fluid structures of Hinduism, the **priests** provide a framework based on social and ritual hierarchy and the scriptures. The **ascetics** represent the freedom of those who have given up the world. A third group of leaders have authority because of their spiritual experience, which enables them to teach and guide others. They are the **gurus**.

The gurus

The gurus span the whole spectrum of Hindu life and practice. Some are Brahmin priests; some are leaders of monastic orders or ascetics. Some are spiritual guides to a few people who are drawn to them, while others attract thousands or even millions of followers. We have seen the role of gurus outside India (chapters 2 and 3).

The concept of gurus goes back at least as far as the *Upanishads*, where the wise pass on knowledge to those who wish to learn. The *Bhagavad Gita* recognises the role of the 'spiritual master': 'Just try to learn the truth by approaching a spiritual master. Inquire from him submissively and render service unto him. The self-realised soul can impart knowledge unto you because he has seen the truth.'[7]

In the centuries that followed, people were looking for alternatives to the social restrictions of caste and the priests who controlled access to the scriptures. The *bhakti* movements, as well as the *tantric* groups, emphasised the role of the guru, often with new and radical teaching.

In the twentieth century gurus have become important again and their numbers have multiplied. One reason for their popularity may be the pressure of contemporary life.[8] Secularism and materialism have eroded people's confidence in traditional religion. But they are still looking for answers to spiritual questions. Gurus can make spiritual truth simple and clear. They can make religion personal, even tangible. They can deal with contemporary problems or explain the scriptures in ways that make sense for today. A businessman was sitting on his veranda in Mombasa when a guru from the Nirankari sect came by. They began to talk about spiritual matters and the guru answered the businessman's questions in a few simple sentences. From that moment he set aside all other aspects of Hinduism and followed only the Nirankari as his guru.

Most gurus have developed their own framework for explaining Hinduism, selecting from a range of complex ideas. They put it across in simple and memorable ways, using homely illustrations. Many have combined ideas from other faiths and quote from Sikh, Buddhist or Christian scriptures. Some gurus are regarded as actual incarnations of God, while others are recognised as souls who have realised the truth in their experience. Some gurus claim to take on their students' *karma* and ensure that they will reach *moksha*, if not in this life, then at least in the next one or two.

Whatever the message, it is important to accept the authority of the guru: 'It is necessary to select a person to whom we can surrender ourselves. Of course no one likes to 'surrender to anyone.'[9]

Bhagwan Rajneesh used to give daily lectures at his *ashram* in Pune. Those who wished to enter could not bring in anything made of leather, since Rajneesh was allergic to leather. There was a large sign at the entrance 'Leave your shoes and your mind here'.

Rajneesh was serious. His aim was to 'kill the mind'. He told his followers to give up their attempts to find God or truth through thinking: '*Dharma* has nothing to do with thoughts or thinking. It has to do with *not-thinking*. Thinking is philosophy. It does give you results or conclusions but does not give you satisfaction.'[10] Rather his disciples should simply follow his instructions in order to experience enlightenment, through a combination of meditation, psychological and physical exercises, group dynamics or sexual activity.

People consult their guru before making a journey or starting a new business venture. A businesswoman was all set to leave on a trip to India, when her guru told her not to come because the date was not auspicious. Naturally, she postponed her plans.

Some gurus demonstrate their authority through miracles. The most famous of the miracle gurus is Satya Sai Baba, whose miracles include producing objects out of thin air, healing the sick and knowing the thoughts of his disciples, wherever they are in the world. Long lists of miracles have been documented. While some have been explained by other experts as examples of conjuring, not all can apparently be explained in this way. Sai Baba is claimed to have fifty million followers around the world.

The absolute control which some of the gurus exercise has not gone unchallenged by others. Swami Dayanand Saraswati, who lectures around the world, describes it as manipulation and co-dependency: 'There are some gurus who want to be in control, and some people who want to be totally dependent. They meet each other's needs.'[11]

Most Hindus are realistic in their attitude to gurus. They are willing to recognise spiritual authority where it is found but are suspicious of those who ask for money first.

The role of women
The role of women in Hinduism, as in other religions, has been ambivalent. The way that women have been seen, both in scripture and in law and practice, has varied greatly. Many goddesses are worshipped, but their character is seen in different ways. On the one hand they represent the provision and protection of a mother, a source of fertility and strength. But they also represent unpredictability and forces that can be destructive.

In traditional Hindu thought a woman's *dharma* was to be subject to her husband and provide him a son to continue the family line. If she 'failed' in this she might be seen to be evil, and certainly acting against her *dharma*. The role of the widow was particularly unfortunate in Hindu society. Girls were destined for marriage and home and so their education was neglected until comparatively recently.

At the same time women have always enjoyed considerable power and influence in society. The *Ramayana* opens with the traditional *Svayambhara* ceremony, where a princess chose her own husband – the one strong enough to bend the bow and win her hand. In modern times, India was one of the first three countries to have a woman Prime Minister and women were given equal rights in law in 1953, at least twenty years before similar legislation in the UK.

Within the practice of Hinduism, women's role is crucial. They carry out the rituals at home and often do much of the voluntary work for temple worship. It could be argued that women provide the real structure of Hinduism by maintaining the rituals that keep the family together. Whatever people believe or not, it is these rituals and family structure that keep them within Hinduism.

Pandita Ramabai, the daughter of a Brahmin priest and a great social reformer, summed up the paradoxical place of women in Hinduism at the end of the nineteenth century: 'I doubt whether charitable institutions could go on at all were it not for women. When women go to hear a Purana or to worship God in a temple, they never go empty-handed . . . And yet, in spite of that, Hinduism declares that women are compounded of every evil thing in the universe.'[12]

Hindu women usually wear a red dot on their forehead (called *tika* or *tilak* or *bindi*). This is made of red powder (*sindhur*), applied to the forehead with the fourth finger. Some also put *sindhur* in the parting of their hair. Among other things, it is the symbol of a married woman and not worn by widows or unmarried girls. These days it is more of a fashion accessory and the colour can vary to suit your outfit. A few years ago a rather nasty gang in a US city called themselves 'dot-busters' and set out to harass Asian women because they resented the success of the Asian community.

It is a question whether women can achieve *moksha*. In the *Bhagavad Gita* Krishna says that even low caste people, Sudras and women can attain the highest state if they take refuge in him.[13] This might imply that *moksha* is usually available even to such people, or it may mean that this is an exceptional example of grace. It seems more likely that this is an exception. The rule is that women and people of lower castes need to progress through the cycle of birth and rebirth to achieve a state in which they are ready for *moksha*.

Leaders in the Diaspora

As Hindus have settled outside India, community leaders have become important figures. As we saw in chapter 3, the first organisations to be established were not temples but 'Indian organisations' for cultural and social needs, followed by caste and ethnic organisations. Their leaders, often prominent business people, have maintained continuity and provided for the spiritual nurture of their communities. For example, they might sponsor a series of religious lectures by visiting teachers. Priests at the temples are usually brought over from India, on a limited contract for one or two years. They have an important role in teaching and leading rituals, but the leadership of the communities is in the hands of the local leaders.

Some of the social and cultural associations have become very influential. For example, the annual dinner of the Lohana Society, a caste association, attracts most of the UK's top Asian businessmen as well as senior government ministers. It is a place to see and be seen, to do business and make contacts.

The *Directory of Religions in the UK*[14] lists nearly five hundred Hindu social, cultural and religious groups, including places of worship. As always, cultural, social and religious functions are blended. Worship can be conducted at any of these places, while temples can also be places of community activity. Business Link London is planning to use the temple network as a way of getting in touch with Asian business people.

Weddings are important social occasions, when families get together, renew contacts with relatives and friends, look out for suitable marriage partners for their young people, and so maintain their cultural and religious community.

There are a number of umbrella bodies, for example the National Council for Hindu Temples in the UK. Attempts are being made to bring these different bodies together into an overall association of all Hindu organisations in the UK.

Religion and politics

During the first forty years of India's independence, most leaders sought to keep religion and politics separate. They saw India as a secular country and wanted to avoid the religious tensions which led to Partition and still erupt in violence between communities. However, the past ten years have seen the increase of Hindu nationalism, expressed in cultural and religious groups like the RSS and the Vishwa Hindu Parishad and the political party which they back – the Bharatiya Janata Party (chapters 2 and 3).

Some religious leaders have been influential in politics. Many politicians consult their astrologer or guru before taking any important decision. Indira Gandhi would often visit the famous Tirupati temple before announcing big policy changes or cabinet appointments. One of the most controversial figures is the 'godman' Chandra Swamy, an influential adviser to Prime Ministers Indira Gandhi and Narsimha Rao. He was often a guest at important political functions, including a charity reception at Downing Street in London, where he was seen reading the palms of several British politicians. Chandra Swamy is currently in prison, facing charges of corruption.

Caste

Caste is still the major fixed structure of Hinduism. Over many centuries it has provided stability and security, as well as a measure of interdependence. It has also been an instrument of oppression and inequality. Many have protested against it, from Buddha to the *bhakti* movements. The last hundred years have seen concentrated efforts by Hindu reformers to abolish caste distinctions, or at least to reform its worst inequalities.

Untouchability

The main focus has been the situation of the Untouchables, the group right outside the system. Dr Karan Singh, a leading Hindu thinker, has described their 'ill treatment over the centuries' as 'a standing disgrace to the otherwise remarkable achievements of Hindu civilisation'.[15]

The Untouchables form about 15 per cent of the population of India. As they had always been excluded from temples and from hearing the scriptures, their religion was one of popular or 'folk' beliefs. Many embraced Buddhism or Islam or joined the *bhakti* sects. At the end of the nineteenth and early twentieth century large numbers became Christian or followed their own gurus like Ravidas in the Punjab or Jagjivan Das, who formed the Satnami movement in Central India.

Mahatma Gandhi spoke out against untouchability and renamed the Untouchables *Harijans**, 'God's people'. After 1935 they were officially known as the Scheduled Castes, because they were listed in a Schedule of those eligible for certain benefits. From the 1970s members of this group have chosen to call themselves *Dalits**, a word which means 'oppressed'.[16]

Gandhi's opposition to untouchability was based on moral conviction, but the matter also became political in the 1920s and 1930s, as the British government announced its intention of separate electorates for different communities. The Untouchables were counted as a separate minority group. The politics of numbers became significant. Dr Ambedkar, the Untouchables' leader, was in favour of a separate electorate, while Gandhi bitterly opposed it and undertook a 'fast unto death' to end untouchability and keep the *Harijans* within the Hindu community. The Poona Pact was signed in September 1932 between caste Hindus and Untouchable leaders. It gave them reserved seats within a common electorate. Gandhi continued to fight to allow them access to temples, wells and public places. He wanted to keep the caste *system* but change the *attitudes* of caste Hindus.

The 1950 Constitution of India, of which Ambedkar was the chief architect, abolished untouchability and all forms of discrimination based on it. It took affirmative action by providing a quota of reservations for the Scheduled Castes in education, employment, Parliament and State Legislatures. The result, over fifty years of independence, has been a marked change in their status and access to all areas of life. However, this has produced a backlash, especially in some rural areas where discrimination has persisted. Many Dalits were (and are) landless labourers in a semi-feudal system. The former landlords have not appreciated the change in their status and there have been many acts of violence against Dalits.

Some still choose religious conversion as a way to change. In 1956 Dr Ambedkar became a Buddhist, along with thousands of his followers. In 1981 some two thousand Dalits became Muslims in a number of villages around Meenakshipuram in South India (chapter 9). Others have become Christians in different places.

In Britain, people from lower castes still feel excluded and several thousand have recently converted to Buddhism.[17] 'Why do we call ourselves Hindus?' asked Arun Kumar from Luton, 'They haven't given us anything. They have humiliated us and they try to humiliate us now. They never treated us as equals. So that is why I'm going to some different religion. Buddhism is best for Indians, because everybody treats us as equal. I've got self-respect.' Som Lal, a Brahmin priest, argued that caste was not part of the Hindu religion but a device of Brahmins 'to keep their supremacy'.

In Jamkhed, a backward area in Western India, village people express very similar feelings as a result of their involvement with the Comprehensive Rural Health Project led by Drs Raj and Mabelle Arole: 'Before we were afraid of the people from higher castes. But now we have dignity – we know that we are human beings, made in the image of God.'[18]

'Other Backward Classes'

In recent years the focus has shifted from the Dalits to the much larger group of Sudras, the fourth caste in the Varna system. These are known as the 'Other Backward Classes' (OBCs) and form 45 to 50 per cent of the population of India. They see themselves squeezed between the upper castes, who have maintained their hold over politics, education and employment, and the Dalits, who have benefited from extensive reservations.

Of course there are great differences in the position of the hundreds of groups in this enormous category. Some have followed a policy of upward mobility, called 'sanskritisation'. They have assimilated themselves with the higher castes, by adopting practices and even caste names that align them with the mainstream. Others have moved in the opposite direction and exploited their differences by forming voting blocks or political parties based on caste. The result has been polarisation. In Bihar, for centuries the most feudal state in India, power is now held by Laloo Prasad Yadav, who heads a party consisting of Yadavs, a caste group from the middle of the OBCs. (They were originally cattle herders and milk-men.) In the neighbouring state of Uttar Pradesh, India's largest, the battle lines are drawn between upper castes (represented by the BJP), OBCs and Dalits. They may choose to stick together to keep out the BJP, but there is little love lost between them. The 1996 elections in India were fought almost entirely on caste or regional lines.

'In the 1930s the battle over untouchability was a matter of ritual purity and pollution,' says Andre Beteille, a prominent Indian sociologist. 'Today the violence between different caste groups is based on their struggle for economic and political power, especially in situations where resources are scarce.'[19]

The Mandal Commission

In 1990 the government of India accepted the recommendations of a commission headed by a judge called Mandal. The Mandal Commission recommended substantial increases in reservations for members of the Other Backward Classes in education and jobs. The OBCs welcomed the decision but in Delhi and other cities a succession of upper caste students committed suicide. They despaired of ever getting jobs in an already tight employment market. The suicides sparked off rioting and in the end the government resigned.

Mandal and *Mandir*

The new government managed to put the issue on the back burner by appointing a committee and postponing implementation. At one point it was facing two burning issues: '*Mandal*' and '*Mandir*'. '*Mandir*' (temple) referred to the temple at Ayodhya which the Hindu nationalists were campaigning to build, on the site of the Babri Masjid Muslim mosque. The destruction of the mosque caused further rioting.

Mandal and *Mandir* illustrate the tension between those who want to go back to the glories of the past Hindu cultural heritage, along with its social order, including caste, and those who are pressing for change. Social tensions are found everywhere, not just in India. The dilemma here is that the caste system is not just any old structure that has evolved, but one which is at the heart of Hinduism.

Reflection

Hinduism sits light to structure. There is no centralised priesthood or administrative hierarchy. The person with spiritual experience or power commands respect and can gain a following. *Sadhus* (ascetics) represent the ultimate escape from all structure. In one way Hinduism is the most individualistic religion in the world. Each individual must work out his or her path to salvation.

At the same time, Hinduism is held together tightly by the social structure of family and caste. People are free to believe and practise (almost) anything – so long as they stay within the bounds of this social framework. This is as true in the villages, where group pressure is strong, as in the sophisticated environments of highly educated communities in India and the Diaspora. It is only in the daily round of city life that the outward restrictions of caste practice have almost disappeared. The inner ties remain.

1. The *Laws of Manu* 1.93.
2. The *Laws of Manu* 6.49.
3. From a devotional song by Kabir (1440–1518).
4. Sunder Raj, *The Confusion called Conversion* (TRACI, New Delhi, 1988), p. 92.
5. The judgement was given by the Kerala High Court and reported in *The Hindu*, a national newspaper published in Madras, 5 December 1995.
6. *Telegraph Magazine*, February 1989.
7. *Bhagavad Gita* 4.34.
8. There is a full discussion of this in Vishal Mangalwadi's book

The World of Gurus (Cornerstone Press, Chicago, 1992).

9. A. C. Bhaktivedanta Swami Prabhupada, *Raja Vidya: The King of Knowledge* (The Bhaktivedanta Book Trust, Germany, 1993), p. 74.
10. Vishal Mangalwadi, *The World of Gurus*, p. 89.
11. In a lecture at the Bharatiya Vidya Bhavan, London, June 1996.
12. In a Marathi book which she published in Bombay in 1889, quoted by Nicol MacNicol, *The Story of Pandita Ramabai, a Builder of Modern India* (1926, reprinted by Nivedita Good Books, 1996).
13. *Bhagavad Gita* 9.32.
14. Paul Weller (ed.), *Religions in the UK: A Multi Faith Directory* (Inter-Faith Network for the United Kingdom, 1993).
15. Karan Singh, *Essays on Hinduism* (Ratna Sagar, Delhi, 1990), p. 9.
16. Useful information on these issues is found in Gerald Larson, *India's Agony over Religion* (State University of New York Press, Albany, 1995); Arthur Bonner, *Averting the Apocalypse* (Duke University Press, 1990); John Webster, *The Dalit Christians: a History* (ISPCK, Delhi, 1992).
17. 'Casualties of the Caste System in Britain', in Radio Five Live's *Asian Perspective* programme, 8 March 1997.
18. Mabelle and Rajnikant Arole, *Jamkhed* (Macmillan, 1994).
19. *East*, BBC2 programme, March 1996.

9

Propagating the Faith

Let noble thoughts come from every side. Rig Veda

The highest truth needs no communicating
for it is by its very nature self-propelling.
It radiates its influence silently
as the rose its fragrance. Mahatma Gandhi

Vedanta and vedanta alone can become the universal
religion of man. Swami Vivekananda[1]

Hinduism has often been described as the most tolerant of
all religions. And this is true of the vast majority of Hindus.
They believe with all sincerity that all ways of belief are
equally valid. If you visit a Hindu temple or cultural association you will be warmly welcomed, invited to see what
goes on and invited back. You will be struck by the sincerity
and warmth of devotion. 'Hindus believe that there are no
heathens or enemies and that everyone has a right to evolve
spiritually and realise the truth in time.'[2]

Swami Vivekananda frequently referred to this: 'The
Christian is not to become a Hindu or Buddhist, nor a Hindu
or Buddhist to become a Christian. But each must assimilate
the spirit of the others and yet perceive his individuality and
grow according to his own law of growth.'[3]

Behind this lies the view that all truth is one, though we
perceive it in different ways. Swami Pramukh of the Swaminarayan mission says that the truth belongs to everybody:
'What is good is mine, not what is mine is good.'

Each of us must pursue our own path: 'Your way is very good for you, but not for me. My way is good for me, but not for you. My way is called in Sanskrit my *ishtam*. Mind you, we have no quarrel with any religion in the world. We have each our *ishtam*.'[4]

V. Krishnamurthy goes so far as to say:

Why should one become a Hindu? What is so great in Hinduism, which Jesus did not preach or Prophet Mohammed did not propagate? Hinduism says: if you are a Christian, be a good Christian. By being a good Christian, you are more of a good Hindu than one who has been born in the religion of Hinduism, and does not have the right attitude to other ways of believing in God. Hinduism is a question of attitudes rather than any physical or formal belonging. In fact this is the main reason why Hinduism never cared about conversions into it from another religion.[5]

Hindus have no problem about learning about other faiths, attending their worship, or sending their children to Sunday School. Many Hindu families in East Africa used to have Christian *ayahs* (maids) for their children, who taught them Bible stories. Chandu Malkani, a London businessman who serves as a priest of his community, goes to church every Christmas to express his 'reverence for Jesus Christ'. He feels that if people could only realise that all religions are seeking the same goals, there would be no need for tension between them.

A missionary religion?
This attitude of tolerance and openness is widespread. In that case, do Hindus consider it necessary to spread their faith? Christians and Muslims have always believed that they have a duty to spread their faith (though by rather different methods). Buddhists have vigorously propagated their beliefs. And there are many other religious groups that work hard to make converts. By comparison, Hinduism does not appear to be a 'missionary' religion.

But when we look more closely, we find that there are several attitudes among Hindus to the idea of propagating their faith. The *Directory of Religions in the UK* states that 'generally Hindus do not engage in activity aimed at converting non Hindus to Hinduism, but they do seek to promote the *Sanatana Dharma* among all people'.[6]

The picture is more complex than it first appears and in some ways paradoxical. Here are some of the factors that make up Hindus' attitudes to other faiths.

1. *Hindus remember the impact of other religions and their attempt to convert Hindus in the past.*

The Muslim invasions of India began from the tenth century and continued over the next 400 years. Significant numbers of Hindus became Muslims, some under pressure. Today Muslims form 10 per cent of the population of India. The proportion was much higher before Partition in 1947, when there were large Muslim majorities in the areas which are now Pakistan and Bangladesh.

Christians have been in India since at least the third century and probably since the first. Many believe that the apostle Thomas, one of Jesus' twelve disciples, arrived in 70 AD on the coast of what is now Kerala and preached across South India, being martyred near Madras. When Roman Catholic missionaries came in the sixteenth century they found an established Christian community in Kerala. They were followed by Protestant missionaries from the seventeenth century onward.

Contrary to popular opinion, the colonial powers did little to help Christian missionaries. It is true that the Portuguese authorities in Goa exerted pressure on the local people to be converted. But elsewhere, Roman Catholic missionaries like Francis Xavier preached freely and found a ready response, especially from the fishermen of the south coast. The East India Company actively opposed any Christian missionary activity. The traders saw a threat to their commercial gain in any social, cultural or spiritual disturbance. They wanted to keep the status quo. William Carey, one of the early Protestant missionaries, who arrived in 1793, was not allowed to land in Calcutta and began work in the nearby Danish settlement of Serampore. It was not until 1813 that missionaries were allowed to enter the territory of the East India Company, which now covered most of India.

At the end of the nineteenth century, when many thousands of Untouchables became Christians, it was assumed that the motivation was for material benefit. There is no doubt that they were looking for change from their oppressed position at the bottom of the ladder. However, the moral and spiritual transformation of these communities was remarkable.

Hindus look back and see a history of conversion from Hinduism. This is the background of Dr Karan Singh's comments to a gathering of Hindus in the USA:

> Our Sastras teach us to respect all religions; all we expect in return is equal respect from the followers of other religions. One thing has to be made clear, and that is that Hinduism is no longer prepared to be on the receiving end of aggressive proselytization. There is no longer going to be a one-way traffic . . . The day has gone when Hinduism was like some helpless whale being constantly bitten into by aggressive sharks.[7]

2. Hindus feel distress when people leave Hinduism, because they are seen as betraying their family and culture.

As we saw, the basic definition of a Hindu is somebody born into a Hindu family. *Dharma* means fulfilling your role in your family and community. It is bound up with the rituals and customs that keep a family together. So if you say that you want to join a different faith, it is not just a private matter of belief. In that case, there are plenty of options within the Hindu system. You are seen as leaving your community and joining another one, which is very painful. There is no concept of apostasy in Hinduism as in Islam. But to leave your family and community is a betrayal. Prakash went back to visit his family, after becoming a follower of Christ. His elder brother made him wait for a long time outside. Finally he asked, 'How could you reject your parents? Your father and mother are your gods. How could you worship another god?'

The early converts to Islam removed themselves from their former social and cultural links. They renounced caste and took new names. In many cases they transferred their allegiance to a new ruler, either forcibly or willingly. In the case of Christians the process was not so extreme. But some converts broke their caste rules and associated with people of other castes. Baptism and participation in the Holy Communion were seen as symbols of belonging to a new community. Many (not all) took new names.

In reaction, some Hindu families regarded the person converted as cut off. Some held funeral services for their dead relative. In such cases the converts, cut off from their former social and cultural group, were forced to depend on the missionaries and live inside their compounds. Separate communities grew up, developing their own distinct culture, no longer a part of the mainstream Hindu society. If people became Christians in groups, they could carry their cultural identity with them. This happened in some cases, especially with the large-scale movements of the Untouchables and lower castes. But they were already on the margins of Hindu society.

So Hindus have seen conversion very much as a social and cultural dislocation, more than spiritual change. They do not separate religion and culture. Many assume that all Europeans and North Americans are Christians and that what they see of Western culture, through TV, films and advertising, is Christian. There is some truth in this, as Christianity has had a profound impact on Western culture and its heritage is still very evident. But much of modern Western culture has explicitly rejected Christian beliefs and practices. However, the idea that a person can separate personal religious beliefs from cultural and social links is foreign to Hindu *dharma*, which is community-based.

3. *As Hindus have come in contact with people of other faiths, some have expressed the view that Hinduism is the broadest, most ancient system of belief and therefore superior to others.*

'Even those who are devoted to other gods and worship them with faith are really worshipping Me, though not in the proper way.'[8] These words of Krishna express tolerance and acceptance of other faiths and ways to God. But they can also imply that they are less than the best.

Swami Vivekananda preached that all religions are equally valid ways to God. Each person must follow their own way. But he also taught that these different ways are stages. At a lower stage is the worship of many gods, through images. A higher stage is the person who believes in one personal God. The highest level is the realisation of the Absolute as the eternal impersonal principle, the One Reality. For him *Advaita Vedanta* was the highest form of religion. He felt it was truly universal, because it was based on universal principles, rather than the limited personality of a historical founder.

Sarvepalli Radhakrishnan took the same view. He saw mystical experience, the realisation of the One, as the 'eternal religion behind all religions, this *sanatana dharma*, the timeless tradition . . . Our historical religions have to transform themselves into the universal faith or they will fade away.'[9]

The same idea is implied by those who affirm the superiority of Indian culture and spirituality: 'Hindu *dharma* is the world's oldest living religion, over 8500 years old,' says the exhibition on 'Understanding Hinduism' at the Swaminarayan Temple in Neasden. 'Hindu *dharma* existed many years before the civilisations of Egypt and China and before the rise of the Roman Empire. There is also evidence of Hindu astronomers mapping the skies, doctors performing surgery and seers composing scriptures before Western civilisation.' The exhibition describes the achievements of early Indian culture in language, education, mathematics (the zero and the decimal system), geometry, astronomy and surgery. This justifiable pride in the Indian heritage is linked for many with the idea that Hindu *dharma,* which lies behind it, has superior value and worth.

Diaspora Hindus – like any immigrant community – want to maintain their identity in their host country. For the first generation it is the struggle to survive and establish themselves. After that it is the concern to teach the children and grandchildren their roots and the heritage of their culture, language, arts, music and religion. As we have seen,

Hinduism brings all these together in a way of life. That is why the temples and the cultural associations are involved in such a wide range of activities. Maintaining your religion is part of maintaining your cultural identity. Anything which threatens that identity is negative. Changing your beliefs would be seen by many as one of those threats.

4. *Hinduism has been a missionary, propagating religion in the past.*

In chapter 3 we saw how Hinduism spread, along with Buddhism, to the countries of South East Asia. Much of the work was done by Brahmins who travelled to other countries to teach and establish their faith. Their expansion coincided with the spread of trade and culture. For example, Hindu beliefs and worship had been part of Nepal from a very early time, but there were certain periods when the caste system and social structure were established by Brahmin priests. These movements were often encouraged by particular groups or individuals who had come to power and reinforced their position with religious sanctions.[10]

D. S. Sarma comments: 'History shows that Hinduism in its days of strength took into its fold unhesitatingly thousands of men and alien tribes and nations.'[11]

5. *Neo-Hinduism today is a missionary, propagating religion.*

The last hundred years have seen further changes in Hinduism, resulting in some vigorous attempts to propagate itself.

The reform movements

The nineteenth century reform movements had two emphases. One was social reform within Hinduism – removing superstitions and unjust practices that had come in. The other was a strong attempt to bring back Hindus who had become Muslims or Christians. The *Arya Samaj* led the way with two major programmes: *shuddhi* and *sanghatan*.

Shuddhi was a purification ceremony for people to come back to Hinduism. Thousands who had become Muslims or Christians were reconverted in the nineteenth and early twentieth centuries. Untouchables and tribals were also given the opportunity to enter the Hindu fold.

Sanghatan was the programme for organising Hindus for self-defence. It encouraged them to speak out against the opponents of Hinduism, especially Islam and Christianity. 'This militant spirit of the *Samaj* has introduced into Hindu society a tone of manliness and sense of self respect which it had lost during the centuries of Muslim rule.'[12]

Swami Vivekananda and the Ramakrishna Mission also worked to propagate Hinduism, though in a different way from the *Arya Samaj*. Swami Vivekananda wanted the regeneration of Indian society through renunciation, service, social reform and teaching the religious truths of Hinduism to the masses. His ideal was a religion of strength, not weakness. At the same time the Ramakrishna Mission became active in spreading Hinduism – especially Vedanta – in other countries, following Swami Vivekananda's successful visits to the United States and Europe.

The gurus and the nationalists

As we have already seen, neo-Hinduism in the twentieth century has been led by the gurus and the nationalists.

The gurus: Hinduism without Indian culture? Many of the gurus have been vigorously engaged in propagating Hinduism, both in India and around the world. They have been skilful communicators and some have backed their words with miraculous claims. Their message has been open to all, without the need to adopt Indian culture or become a part of the social structure of Hinduism.

The nationalists: Hinduism as Indian culture? The nationalists have promoted Hinduism based on Indian culture. Their message has been that Hinduism is the basis of Indian culture and Indian culture is the glory of Hinduism. Their goal has been clear – to restore the glorious heritage of the past through the acceptance of Hindu values.

The major force behind Hindu nationalism is the RSS, the *Rashtriya Swayamsevak Sangh* (National Voluntary Society), founded in 1925. It has around 750,000 volunteers, organised in about 30,000 *shakas* (branches) across India and other countries (100 in the UK). The volunteers meet regularly for drill and practice in martial arts. They are trained to help in emergencies and also for self-defence. The RSS is a cultural organisation – but the word *cultural* includes every aspect of society, social, moral, economic, political and spiritual. The RSS pledge makes this clear: 'In the name of God and of my ancestors, I hereby become a member of the *Rashtriya Swayamsevak Sangh* for the all-round progress of *Bharat-varsha* by strengthening the holy *Hindu Dharma*, *Hindu Sanskriti* and *Hindu Samaj*. *BHARAT MATA KI JAI*.'[13]

The Supreme Court recently argued that the words *Hindu*, *Hinduism* or *Hindutva* (a Hindu state) are not merely religious but also refer to India's culture and heritage. Not everybody will agree with this argument but it illustrates again how closely these ideas are linked.

The RSS has attracted extremes of praise and criticism from other Hindus. The discipline and dedication of its volunteers have been much admired. They are usually the first on the scene of floods, famine or other disasters. But its identification of Hinduism with Indian nationalism has made it appear intolerant and fanatical. M. S. Golwalkar, one of its leading ideologues, argued that non-Hindus in India were 'foreigners' who must 'adopt the Hindu culture and language, must learn to respect and hold in reverence Hindu religion . . . and must lose their separate existence to merge in the Hindu race'.[14]

Mahatma Gandhi was assassinated by a member of the RSS who believed he had betrayed the Hindu cause to the Muslims. As a result the RSS was banned for a number of years but had re-emerged by the 1970s. The RSS works through other organisations like the *Vishwa Hindu Parishad* (World Hindu Organisation) and the *Bharatiya Janata* Party (Indian People's Party). Some of these groups work in states like Madhya Pradesh to re-convert people – mostly tribals – who have become Christians. Several thousand are reported to have been re-converted.[15]

What do Hindus think about mission by others?
Hindus have been exposed in India to a range of religions with different attitudes to propagating their faith.

Buddhists and Jains

Buddhism and Jainism started as reform and protest movements. Their followers were opposed and sometimes persecuted. The Jains have continued as a separate group with a distinct identity, though very much part of the Hindu cultural tradition. The Buddhists were re-absorbed into Hinduism. The philosopher Sankara provided a philosophical alternative and many were won back by the spiritual enthusiasm of the *bhakti* movements. Buddhism virtually disappeared within India until this century when Dr Ambedkar, the leader of the Untouchables (Dalits), became a Buddhist, along with thousands of his followers. Today there are about 5 million Buddhists in India, usually known as Neo-Buddhists because of their recent origin.

Sikhs

The Sikh religion started from the teaching of Nanak, a *bhakti* leader with a monotheistic doctrine of God and rejection of castes and images. Sikhs were seen as a sect of Hinduism and it was nearly two hundred years before they became a separate religious and political group, organised into a military brotherhood in order to survive under Muslim persecution. Sikhs and Hindus have lived together with a great deal of interlinking. Some Hindu families give one of their sons to become a Sikh and marry into a Sikh family, and vice versa. Recent extremist movements for a separate Sikh nation have created tension between Hindus and Sikhs in Punjab, but this is political rather than religious.

Many Hindus use the Sikh scriptures, while Sikhs regularly visit Hindu temples. At the Vedic Temple in Southampton, large numbers of Sikh women attend the worship of the goddess Durga, often through the night. 'On those days you will find a big pile of fruit and coconuts in front of her shrine,' the temple secretary explains. 'They find that Durga has power to answer their prayers.'

Sikhs, along with Buddhists and Jains, are seen as part of the Hindu family. People from their lower economic and social groups in India receive the same privileges as Hindu Scheduled Castes.

Muslims

Hindus on the whole regard Islam as a religion which converted people by force. In fact, there was considerable accommodation between Hindus and Muslims in the early centuries. They adapted to each other's social life and customs. The Muslim mystics or Sufis had a lot in common with Hindu spirituality and philosophy. Kabir (1440–1518) was a Muslim weaver who combined Hindu ideas with the rejection of caste, idol worship and the authority of the *Vedas*. The Emperor Akbar tried to establish a universal religion combining elements of Islam, Hinduism and Christianity, but it did not last beyond his death. During the twentieth century Muslims and Hindus moved apart until the climax of Partition in 1947, resulting in terrible bloodshed and millions of refugees. Muslims and Hindus on the whole live separately today, with tensions which flare up from time to time, especially in places where there are crowded populations, competing for scarce resources.

In 1982 two thousand Hindus from the Scheduled Castes (Dalits) became Muslims in a group of villages near Meenakshipuram in South India. The event caused a stir and groups of RSS volunteers came to try to re-convert them, as well as to meet the social needs of other lower caste Hindus. There were outcries in the press and many were convinced that there must have been foreign money from Arab Muslim countries to finance the conversions. The converts themselves, including a few Christians who had joined them, professed satisfaction that they were now free from caste oppression.

Christians

Hindu attitudes to Christian mission cover a wide spectrum. Hindus generally have great reverence for the figure of Jesus and willingly accept him as an incarnation or manifestation of God, along with others. Many have incorporated Christian beliefs and values into their Hindu framework. Mahatma Gandhi's favourite hymns were 'Lead Kindly Light' and 'When I Survey The Wondrous Cross'.

In chapter 2 we saw how Christian values and example had a profound impact on the reform movements of the nineteenth century. Since then, others value Christian service through schools, hospitals and other social activities. Mother Teresa is much admired. The 'missionary spirit' is praised. But they would not consider changing their own spiritual and cultural framework.

A small but significant number, both in India and abroad, have become followers of Christ. For others the call to follow Jesus Christ as the only Saviour and Lord is a major stumbling block. In some minds it causes suspicion of Christianity and its 'missionary activity'. In the 1950s the state government of Madhya Pradesh set up the Niyogi Commission to investigate the activities of Christian missionaries. It produced a negative report, which led some years later to the passing of a 'Freedom of religion' Bill in that state and later in Orissa. In both states the law forbids conversion through any kind of inducement or force. People who wish to be baptised may be required to make a statement before the magistrate that their conversion has been voluntary.

A letter to the *Maharashtra Herald* expresses this rather suspicious view:

> The conversions in India have invariably resulted in dissatisfaction, separatism and gradual de-nationalisation of the converts. The attitude of the converts (one of dislike) towards the parental religion, culture and history is very obvious. They may not be very educated, but becoming Christians, it would seem, entitles them to ridicule everything that is Indian ... On the other hand the converts in the West – adopting any sect of Hinduism – tend to become better citizens of their mother country.[16]

The idea that people who become Christians give up their culture is common not only in India but in the Diaspora. When Ramesh told his father that he had decided to follow Christ, he replied 'I suppose now you are going to eat beef, drink whisky and become immoral' – the image which he had of Christians. Ramesh reassured him that he was not planning to do any of these things.

Hindus outside India are of course open to adapt to the

culture of the country they are living in, but do not want to
lose their identity or adopt everything uncritically. They
assume that the culture and religion of the host country are
closely connected, whether they are African, British or
American Christians.

Reflection
What is the Hindu attitude to propagating the faith? There is no
simple answer.

The majority do not see it as necessary. They genuinely believe
that all ways are equally valid. Others agree but affirm that the
Hindu way is in fact the oldest and most universal. And many feel
strongly that it is wrong to change the beliefs in which you were
born and brought up – especially if that means changing your
customs and social relationships. Social and cultural factors are
perhaps more important than spiritual in this conviction.

At the same time, a small but growing number are committed
to spreading Hindu ideas and beliefs (in very different ways) and
rejoice whenever they hear news of another person acknowledging
Hindu *dharma* as the best way.

The close link between culture, social structure and religious
beliefs means that the answer to this question will always be
complex.

1. *Works of Swami Vivekananda*, vol. 3, pp. 182–4.
2. *Understanding Hinduism Exhibition*, Shri Swaminarayan
    Mandir, Neasden, London.
3. *Works*, vol. 1, p. 22.
4. ibid., vol. 3, p. 131.
5. V. Krishnamurthy, *Hinduism for the Next Generation* (Wiley
    Eastern, New Delhi, 1992), p. 80.
6. *Religions in the UK: A Multi Faith Directory* (Inter-Faith
    Network for the United Kingdom, 1993), p. 233.
7. Karan Singh, *Essays on Hinduism* (Ratna Sagar, Delhi, 1990),
    p. 82.
8. *Bhagavad Gita* 9.23.
9. S. Radhakrishnan, *Eastern Religions and Western Thought*
    (London, 1939), pp. 80–1.
10. Dor Bahadur Bista, *Fatalism and Development: Nepal's*

Struggle for Modernisation (Orient Longman, Calcutta, 1991).

11. D. S. Sarma, *Hinduism Through the Ages* (Bharatiya Vidya Bhavan, Bombay, 1989), p. 96.

12. ibid.

13. *Bharat* is the name for India. *Hindu Dharma, Hindu Sanskriti* and *Hindu Samaj* can be translated 'Hindu religion, culture and society'. *BHARAT MATA KI JAI: 'Victory to Mother India'*.

14. M. S. Golwalkar, *We, or Our Nationhood Defined*, first published in 1939 and re-published and re-affirmed in 1979.

15. *India Today*, 31 December 1995.

16. L. B. Pendharkar, 24 October 1987.

10

Concluding Reflections

Asatoma sadgamaya
Tamasoma jyotir gamaya
Mrutyorma amrutam gamaya

From the unreal lead me to the real
From darkness lead me to light
From death lead me to immortality[1]

Hinduism: a world faith

> It is already becoming clear that a chapter which had a
> Western beginning will have to have an Indian ending if it
> is not to end in the self-destruction of the human race ...
> At this supremely dangerous moment in history, the only
> way of salvation for mankind is the Indian way.[2]

Hinduism has become a world faith. In the last hundred years
its influence has again spread outside India, with effects on
the whole range of life.

Politicians, film stars and royal figures consult their astrologers or their gurus. Talking about your *karma* is common-
place, even if you are not quite sure what it means!

Management consultants (the new gurus) tell chief execu-
tives to unlock the potential of the Self within them, while
others explain the benefits of Transcendental Meditation to
relieve stress and clear the mind.

The Natural Law Party, based on the teachings of
Maharishi Mahesh Yogi (TM's founder), contested every
seat in the 1992 Parliamentary elections in Britain. Its

manifesto went to every home in the country.

In Moscow, Russians are practising Vedic fire ceremonies. Some want to go back to the ancient Russian (Indo-European) religion, which was Vedic. They believe that soon there will be more Hindus in Russia than in the West.

In many schools in the UK the Hindu view that all religions are all equally valid has become the basis for their policy on Religious Education. *Diwali* is one of the most popular festivals that children learn about.

University Departments of Theology have renamed themselves 'Religious Studies' or have widened their scope to include a variety of faiths. A major department like Lampeter (University of Wales) aims to have each major faith taught 'from within' by a practitioner of that faith.

Yoga has been popular for a long time as a means of exercise and an aid to meditation. Recently it has been used by doctors to help with people with asthma, arthritis or high blood pressure. Health authorities are looking seriously at 'complementary medicine', including the ancient Ayurvedic system of India. Travel agents offer Ayurvedic package tours to Kerala, which include massage, oils and medicines – Calm Balm Holidays. 'People are shifting to traditional systems because we know it doesn't harm us,' said a London student on one of these tours.

At the religious and spiritual level, the insights of Hinduism have been welcomed by many. We have referred many times to the impact of the gurus. The Festival of Mind, Body and Spirit, the major showcase of New Age trends in the UK, is strongly influenced by Hindu ideas and groups.

In Chicago the 1993 Parliament of the World Religions recalled the dramatic contribution made by Swami Vivekananda at the first Parliament in 1893. L. M. Singhvi, Indian High Commissioner in London, movingly described the deep desire of the participants for 'the creation of a new and humane global community of peoples of different nationalities and origins, ideologies and faiths living together in harmony'.[3] Dr Singhvi, a Jain, received an award for religious understanding from the Archbishop of Canterbury in October 1994.[4]

What is the future of Hinduism?

In the Diaspora, different predictions have been made:

'We will lose 10 per cent of our young people unless we start teaching them,' said a Hindu priest on BBC2's *East* programme in October 1991.

Others point to the churches that have turned into temples, *gurudwaras* or mosques, and predict that Hinduism is more likely to grow. Its ideas will continue to permeate society, while the younger generation of Hindus is keen to rediscover its roots and its cultural and religious identity.

This is not always easy. Recently a girl told her friend: 'At school I'm English, at home I'm a Hindu.' (Notice how culture and religion are linked in her comment.) Unlike their parents, who simply absorbed Hindu tradition, young people need conscious teaching. Some have gone back to India to learn. Temples and cultural associations are developing regular teaching programmes, ranging from classes, discussions and youth camps to CD-Roms with 'Everything you want to know about Ganesh, or Krishna or the Ramayana . . .'

Within India, a Hindu government was in power for twelve days in May 1996. The Bharatiya Janata Party overtook the Congress, with its inclusive platform, for the first time in Independent India. Other parties with an explicit caste basis represent the OBCs (Other Backward Classes) and Dalits. Whoever is in power, the tensions over caste and class will continue.

Options in the global village

In today's global village we have to live out our beliefs and practices side by side. Hindus are in contact with people of other faiths or no faith. How do we get along with each other? There was a time when we could stay in isolation, if we wanted to. But that is not possible today.

Conflict

One response is conflict or confrontation. It's all too easy to list examples – the Crusades, Northern Ireland, the Middle East, the Partition of India and Pakistan, Sri Lanka, Punjab,

Ayodhya . . . But we only have to mention them to realise that this approach is futile. We also realise that most of these conflicts are not about truth but about power or identity, based on economic, social and cultural factors.

Co-existence

A more common approach, in our pluralistic society, is to say that all religions are equally good or bad, because ultimately they are saying and doing the same thing. There is truth in this, because we are all human, with the same needs and aspirations, emotional, psychological, social and spiritual. There are similarities in what we believe and practise. There is a lot we can learn from each other.

The 1993 Parliament of the World Religions called for a 'global ethic' based on core values found in all religions. The delegates 'would have had no difficulty in agreeing with Mahatma Gandhi who said that various religions were as leaves of a tree which might seem different but at the trunk they were one'.[5]

And yet, the question of truth keeps coming back to us. How do we know if the path we have chosen is the true one? Will it lead us to God? Or somewhere else? Climbing a mountain in Manali, North India, I came to a place where paths led in several directions. I asked a young man 'Which is the best way to the top?' His reply was philosophical: 'It's better for each person to find his own way to the top.' I made my choice and thought about what he had said. Did all the paths lead to the top? Surely some were better than others? Suppose I took a wrong turning? What if the mist came down and I slipped over the edge?

Choice

If all religions are equally valid, does this increase our choice or limit it? Can we have the freedom to choose between different faiths – real pluralism with choices based on truth? Can we change, or allow others to change? Choice implies criteria for choosing. We must be able to compare – not in a competitive way but in an honest search for truth. All faiths need to be part of this, opening themselves to scrutiny and the possibility of truth and error, rather than a bland assertion that 'it's all the same'.

Are there any criteria for choice? Before we try to answer that, there are two important things to be said:

Dialogue is between friends. The most important thing, as we examine other faiths, is to make friends. As we get to know each other, and trust each other, we can get behind the stereotypes. We can relate as *people*, rather than just representatives of religious faiths. Then we can share our experiences of God, our questions and doubts, our beliefs and certainties. That is how God relates to us, as people, regardless of our background or status.

Cultural identity is important. Culture and religious identity are closely connected, as we have seen. This is specially true for Hindus. For the great majority their faith is what they learned from their parents and families. It is part of their heritage and identity, linked to food and clothes, music and art, festivals and family rituals.

If you accept the truth of another faith, can you keep your culture? That is not difficult if you are looking at Sikhism, Buddhism or Jainism, which share a common cultural heritage with Hinduism. It is also comparatively easy for a Hindu to have a secular outlook but stay within the Hindu social framework. It's more difficult if you want to follow Islam, with its distinctive cultural heritage.

We could explore further how these and other faiths and world-views relate to Hinduism. But for the rest of this chapter we focus on a Christian perspective.

Can you become a follower of Christ and keep your Asian cultural identity? Rajendra Chandra Das, founder of the Khristpanthi *Ashram* in Varanasi, believed that it was possible. 'The heritage of India, in its spiritual as well as cultural aspect, belongs to the Hindu converts to Christianity as to the Hindu himself.'[6]

Are Christians willing to allow this? For a long time Christianity has been closely linked with European and then American culture. But there is no reason why it should be, since Christ was born in the Middle East and Christians believe that he came to reveal God to people of every culture.

In any case, the majority of Christians today are not from Europe or North America.

What would it mean to understand Christian faith and practice from a Hindu perspective? We shall look at ideas of God, ways of worship and practical living.

What is truth?
First, we must begin further back. How do we know what is true? There are at least three major approaches to this question.

The post-modern supermarket
In our post-modern culture, you can choose anything you want from the shelf. Everything is true – for you. So you are free to believe and practise what you like, and so am I.

But how do we know what is true? The result of this apparent freedom is that nothing is true in any ultimate sense. The post-modern consensus is based on despair. We can't know anything that is absolutely true, because there is no outside reference point.

The Hindu view of Truth
The Hindu view at first sight looks similar. It says that the different ways to God are like leaves on the same tree. There are different ways because we have different temperaments and abilities. We are at different stages. The gods are each *roops* or manifestations of the One God. There is infinite variety, with many stories and many streams, which flow in different directions, though they all reach the sea.

A favourite picture is the blind men trying to describe an elephant:

One felt his ear and said *an elephant is like a fan.*
Another clutched his leg and said *an elephant is like a tree.*
The third felt his tail and said *an elephant is like a rope.*
The fourth pressed his side and said *an elephant is like a wall.*

You could interpret this as the post-modern view: nobody

really knows. But Hindus believe that behind the different manifestations there *is* one ultimate Absolute. Somebody or Something can see the *whole* elephant. But the ultimate One is unknowable and can't be defined in language. We can't say anything positive about it, only *neti, neti,* 'not this, not that'. We can express the mystery of the One with sounds and *mantras* (like OM), or rituals, but we can't describe it in words. So our various attempts to express reality in words are just that – only our incomplete attempts.

The Christian view of Revelation

Christians share the same starting point as Jews and Muslims. They believe in One Absolute Creator God who made the world and all that is in it, including human beings. He is distinct from the world and yet permeates it in loving relationship with his creatures. He is infinite but personal. 'In the beginning God created the heavens and the earth . . . light . . . waters . . . earth . . . living creatures . . . human beings in our image, male and female . . . And it was very good.'[7]

God has revealed Himself. Human beings turned away from God and chose independence. This is the meaning of sin and the source of all our problems. It is not that the material world was in some way defective or that our physical bodies are evil. God made the world good but it was spoiled by the effects of human beings' disobedience. But God did not leave them. God is beyond human knowledge but *chooses* to reveal Himself, in words and actions which demonstrate His character. His actions began with the creation of the world and continued in the special deliverance of the people of Israel from slavery, to live as a model community. God spoke through prophets like Moses, the great lawgiver.

The people of Israel were waiting for God to intervene again, to establish justice and righteousness in the world. Christians believe that God *did* intervene decisively, in Jesus Christ. Jesus showed God's love for people of all backgrounds. He specially welcomed those who were weak and on the margins of society. He was a willing guest in their homes but also made himself available to all. His message of love and forgiveness upset the religious establishment and he was sentenced to a cruel death on the cross. This was not just a political murder but a cosmic sacrifice to deal with the separation between God and humanity. Jesus rose again from the dead and is alive today by his Spirit to all who accept him as Saviour and Teacher. He is the Eternal Teacher, the *Sanatan Satguru*.

The big story. The Bible contains many stories. But it is really *one* big story, *one* decisive moment when God came into the world.

Paul, one of Christ's first followers, was asked by the authorities at Athens to explain why he believed in Jesus and the resurrection. He began his speech by referring to the great devotion of the people of Athens. He had even found an altar dedicated 'to the unknown god'. The Athenians were aware of their limitations. They realised that they could not grasp the full truth about God, so they built an altar admitting their ignorance. Paul declared that this was 'God who made the world and everything in it . . . who gives life and breath and everything else to everyone . . . he created all races of mankind and made them live throughout the whole earth . . . so that they would look for Him . . . Yet God is not far from any one of us, for "in him we live and move and have our being".'[8]

Paul argued that people all around the world were seeking God and had some knowledge of Him, though not complete. But now, he said, God was calling everybody to repentance: 'For he has fixed a day in which he will judge the whole world with justice by means of a man he has chosen. He has given a proof of this to everyone by raising that man from death!'[9]

The turning point. For Christians the resurrection of Jesus is the turning point of history. All the searches and hopes of humanity are focused and fulfilled in that moment.

Of course, this raises the question: why only this time and place? Kosuke Koyama, a Japanese writer living in Thailand, comments that we each live in a particular history: 'No one lives *outside* history. Jesus Christ, the true man, lived in history . . . to be a man means to live in a particular historical situation. *Particular*? Yes. We do not live in some general idea of history. We live in a certain locality and each locality has a history, culture and language.'[10]

So God has to intervene in a *particular* place and time in history, so as to become truly a human being, not just appearing to be one. It is also a mark of consistency that there is one unique intervention, which is the same for all people. As Paul said, this reflects what God has shown us of Himself, rather than the varied and sometimes contradictory ideas that we may have: 'a representation by the art and imagination of man'.[11]

But the coming of Jesus is not limited to that time and place. It is the fulfilment of universal longings and expectations, of experiences and ideas that are pointers to God. He specifically fulfilled the expectations of the Jewish people. But we find similar expectations within Hinduism (and among all human beings). For example: the belief in One God, the belief in sacrifice, the belief that God has come into the world in human form, the desire for a guru, the longing to express devotion for God.

How do we know what is true? Hindus and Christians both answer that we can only know if God reveals the truth. Hindus believe that we can know the truth only in fragmentary form. Christians agree but believe that God has decisively shown Himself in the coming of Jesus: 'No one has ever seen God. The only son, who is the same as God and is at the Father's side, he has made Him known.'[12]

Ideas of God

What ideas do Hindus and Christians have about God? Is there any common ground?

Hindus believe in God as the One Reality, the source and ground of all being. The many gods, the images, the *avataras* (incarnations) are manifestations of the One. Many Hindus worship God as personal and believe they need God's grace to bring them into a state of union and communion with God. For example, the Swaminarayan Mission, following the tradition of the philosopher Ramanuja, teaches that the ultimate goal for the devotee is union with God *and* the guru.

Other Hindus accept this but believe it is not the highest stage. Dr Sarvepalli Radhakrishnan spoke about the stages of religious experience. For him the mystical experience of the Absolute is the highest stage: 'The worshippers of the absolute are the highest rank; second to them are the worshippers of the personal God; then we come to worshippers of incarnations like Rama, Krishna, Buddha; below them are those who worship ancestors, deities and sages; and lowest of all the worshippers of the petty forces and spirits.'[13]

Behind all these ideas of God are the principles of *karma* and *dharma*. These are unchangeable laws that govern the whole universe. There is no escape from their workings, though some gods and gurus have intervened to modify their effects for their worshippers.

Christians also believe that God is the one absolute creator of the universe and all that is in it, the source of all being. They believe that God is personal, though not a limited 'person' like a human being. C. S. Lewis was a scholar at Oxford and Cambridge, the writer of the popular Narnia books for children, and a Christian apologist. He once gave a series of radio talks called 'Beyond Personality': 'A good many people nowadays say, "I believe in a God, but not in a personal God." They feel that the mysterious something which is behind all other things must be more than a person.'[14]

But he points out that although some say that God is beyond personality they 'really think of him as something impersonal: that is as something less than personal'. Lewis argued that the Christian idea is that God is *supra-personal*, personal but also infinite. God is three-personal, the divine family of love. Our human personality reflects God's three-dimensional personality.

Christians believe that the supreme characteristic of God is love. In Jesus Christ, God entered into the world of human beings, becoming human, living, suffering and dying among us, to bring us back to God.

Dr Radhakrishnan regarded this idea of a suffering God, 'the deity with a crown of thorns', as religiously unsatisfying, less than the highest. He felt this because for him humanity is essentially divine. There is nothing to forgive; the basic problem is ignorance. Salvation or liberation means *realising* your divinity. For Christians, salvation means *restoring* our relationship with God, which was broken through our turning away from God, which is the meaning of sin.[15]

December 1992. It was the day after the destruction of the Babri Masjid at Ayodhya. We were travelling from Delhi to Calcutta. The train was quite empty, as a lot of people had cancelled their journey, afraid of violence. The train stopped at Patna and we were informed that it would not go any further, as Howrah station (in Calcutta) was closed because of rioting. We had nowhere to go, so we sat in the train, discussing Ayodhya and what could be done to bring reconciliation. One of the passengers, a young Hindu student, said, 'I really love that Christian idea of forgiveness.'

Christians believe that Jesus' death on the cross broke the power of *karma* and anything else which enslaves us. Paul, the follower of Jesus, explained it like this: 'God forgave us all our sins: he cancelled the unfavourable record of our debts with its binding rules and did away with it completely by nailing it to the cross. And on that cross Christ stripped the spiritual rulers and authorities of their power.'[16]

Martin Luther, the German leader of the reformation in the sixteenth century, said about Jesus: 'We are undone if this man is not God. But now – we have a gracious God.'

Ways of worshipping God

How do we achieve the goal of life? Hindus affirm various ways to salvation or *moksha* (liberation). All believe in the importance of fulfilling your *dharma*. But there are different paths:

- Some emphasise *rituals* like the old Vedic sacrifices, which are still practised today, for example in the *havan* ceremony. Or they offer *puja* to the images of gods, through gifts of fruits and flowers. They keep themselves ritually pure through bathing and diet.
- Others approach God through *devotion*, in prayer, music, or dance, to express their desire for direct experience of God.
- Some believe that God is best worshipped through acts of *service* to others.

● Many practise different kinds of *meditation*, including *yoga* exercises, as a way to realise the presence of God, deep inside themselves.

Christians can agree that all these ways have value, though with a radical qualification. Before we can enter on any of them, we need to be liberated by God from our present condition. In other words, *moksha* (liberation) is the *beginning* of the road, rather than the end of it.

Hindus also testify to their need for God's help and grace. For the Christian, this is the starting point. In our present situation we are cut off from God, because we have turned away from Him to rule our own lives. The results are obvious in the selfishness, pride and greed and violence of our world. We are not able to love God or serve our fellow human beings. We are more interested in pleasing ourselves.

This is a universal experience: 'I know what *dharma* is, but I have no inclination toward it; and I know what evil is too, but I cannot get out of it.'[17]

Many feel trapped by the cycle of birth and re-birth. They do not know how to pay their *karmic debt*. The Apostle Paul spoke of the whole creation 'groaning', subject to 'frustration', very much like *maya*.[18]

Christians believe that in Jesus, God Himself entered our world of *maya*, selfishness and rebellion. By His death and resurrection He paid the debt of our sin and *karma*, and enabled us to begin a new life. This is all the result of God's grace: 'But God's mercy is so abundant, and his love for us is so great, that while we were spiritually dead in our disobedience he brought us to life with Christ. It is by God's grace that you have been saved.'[19]

This is the *beginning* of a journey, a relationship, in fellowship with God. In this journey the ways of worship and devotion, prayer and meditation, service and witness all have their part, as our grateful response to God's love. Christians can learn from Hindus' example of reverence, sacrifice and discipline.

Sacrifice

The Vedic sacrifices are similar to the sacrifices of the people of Israel in the Bible. After Jesus' death and resurrection, his followers realised that he had performed the supreme sacrifice, which fulfilled the old sacrifices and made them no longer necessary. One of the early Christians, writing to new believers from a Jewish background, explained it like this: 'The sacrifices serve year after year to remind people of their sins ... Christ, however, offered one sacrifice for sins, an offering that is effective forever, and he sat down at the right hand side of God.'[20]

Christ's followers are called to offer themselves as 'living sacrifices' and to offer praise to God as our sacrifice through Jesus.[21]

Images

Can images help us to focus our thoughts on God? The early Christians described Jesus as *the* 'image' of God, the *pratiroop* (exact manifestation) of God, the Word through whom God's character is seen: 'He reflects the brightness of God's glory and is the exact likeness of God's own being.'[22]

So his followers focus all their devotion, offerings and meditation on him. Some Christians use pictures or images of Jesus as an aid to devotion, while many do not. But all agree that the most important way to 'visualise' him and know his presence is through reading and meditating on the Scriptures, the Bible. The first part of the Bible looks forward to the coming of 'Messiah' (the Hebrew word for Christ), while the second part describes Jesus' life, teaching, death and resurrection, followed by the life and teaching of his early followers. Christians also experience his presence in worship together, especially when remembering his death and resurrection through the bread and wine, symbolising his body and blood. Jesus said, 'Where two or three come together in my name, I am there with them.'[23]

Meditation

Meditation can be a way to come close to God – but it is important to clarify the goal. It is not to empty the mind, as in *yoga*, or to achieve identification with the Absolute, but rather to focus on the character of God. 'What do you see when you think of God?' a Christian asked a group of his friends. Some described a picture that they 'saw' – a wise or powerful being. But most of them described qualities of God's character – love, greatness, mercy, justice, faithfulness, forgiveness, joy. The Bible is the record of God's character revealed in his words and actions. Christians meditate on God's character and so come close to God.

Worship and culture

Christian worship can take many forms, depending on the culture of the worshippers. In practice, much of it is influenced by Western music and art forms. Wherever you go in the world you may find Christians singing hymns originally written in Europe or North America. But you may also find people using their own music and art, which is much better. In many village churches in India, people remove their shoes, sit on the floor and worship in *bhajans* with their own music and words. There is an urgent need for Christians around the world to find new, local forms to express their worship and devotion to Christ the Lord.

A young student described his experience when he read Jesus' words about prayer in the Gospel of John: 'Ask in my name'.

Suddenly a thought occurred to me, 'Why not pray in Christ's name?' I was horrified at this thought. 'What,' said I, 'should I pray in this name? Why should I pray in His name? I am a Brahmin, a Tiwari, a descendant of the *rishis*, a teacher of the world. Shall I pray in His name? Never.'

But I was face to face with the Lord. He said, 'You have used all your methods. You have tried to be good by your own efforts, through philosophy, through meditation; all this has not worked. Why not try this method? Why not try?'

So I got up from my chair and went to the small room adjacent to my study and knelt there and prayed, 'O Lord, if you are a living Lord, save me from my sins. Save me from myself.' At once I realised that there is a gracious Personality by my side on whom I may repose my feverish head, one who is closer than the closest friend, one who understands, one who is undescribable (*anivarchaniya*).

I knew instantly that my sinful habits and besetting temptations were broken, life became different.[24]

The way of life

Followers of Christ, who have started their journey and fellowship with him, do not suddenly become different from other people. They face the same temptations and pressures – to compromise, to live for self, to forget God. They don't need to change their culture – clothes, ways of eating, names and family links. Tiwari shares his perspective:

'When I decided to be baptised, I did not think that I was "leaving" Hindu society. I thought I was adding something new, something glorious to our Hindu heritage. I wanted to continue to live with my parents, to co-operate with the other Hindus in social service work, to visit temples, etc. I was like those early Christians who met daily at Solomon's porch in the temple.'[25]

What is important is that now Christ's followers want to respond to God's love by worshipping Him and serving others through their family life, daily work, and responsibilities in the larger community. Jesus summed up God's requirements like this:

Love the Lord your God with your all heart, with all your soul, with all your mind, and all your strength . . . Love your neighbour as you love yourself.

And now I will give you a new commandment: love one another. As I have loved you, so you must love one another.[26]

As Jesus' followers try to live a life of love they are not alone. Jesus is present with them, living in each disciple by his Spirit. So they are part of God's family of love, entering into the life of eternal union with God, which begins now.

Truth alone will triumph
Satyam Eva Jayate ('Truth alone will triumph') is a motto of Hindus. This chapter – and book – is about truth. Hindus, Christians, people of all faiths or no faith, are all searching for the truth.

We will find it as we listen to each other and share honestly our experiences of seeking God, as well as our failures. We need to listen to those who claim to have found the truth. We must look critically at what they say and compare it with the evidence of their character and actions. Not all are necessarily reliable guides to God and truth. We cannot deny their *experience* but we have a right to ask questions about the *meaning* of that experience. Was it an experience of God or of self? Does it make them more loving? Does it match the character of God as revealed to us from other sources?

Above all we need to listen to God Himself and what He has revealed to us through His Word.

When we have asked these questions, then we can test it for ourselves.

One of India's greatest poets, Rabindranath Tagore, prayed for himself and his country:

Where the mind is without fear and the head held high;
Where knowledge is free;
Where the world has not been broken up into fragments
     by narrow domestic walls;
Where words come out from the depth of truth;
Where tireless striving stretches its arms toward perfection;
Where the clear stream of reason has not lost its way into
     the weary desert sand of dead habit;
Where the mind is led forward by thee into ever widening
     thought and action –
Into that heaven of freedom, my Father, let my country
     awake.[27]

Tagore was greatly influenced by the poetic Bauls of Bengal, a group who were searching for direct encounter with God:

Ah, where am I to find Him, the Man of my heart?

Alas, since I lost Him, I wander in search of Him
Through lands near and far.'[28]

Jesus said, 'I am the way, the truth and the life.'[29]

1. An ancient prayer from the *Vedas*, the earliest Hindu scrip-
    tures.
2. Arnold Toynbee, quoted in the exhibition *Understanding
    Hinduism* at the Shri Swaminarayan Mandir in London.
3. 'A Tale of Three Cities', a lecture about three global confer-
    ences: on ecology, human rights and world religions.
4. The Interfaith Medallion of the International Council of
    Christians and Jews, presented at Lambeth Palace.
5. L. M. Singhvi, *A Tale of Three Cities*.
6. H. L. Richard (ed.), *R. C. Das, Evangelical Prophet for
    Contextual Christianity* (ISPCK, Delhi, 1995).
7. Genesis 1:1–31.
8. Acts of the Apostles 17:24–8.
9. Acts of the Apostles 17:31.
10. Kosuke Koyama, *Water Buffalo Theology* (SCM Press,
    London, 1974), p. 43.
11. Acts of the Apostles 17:29.
12. Gospel of John 1:18.
13. S. Radhakrishnan, *The Hindu view of life* (1927), p. 18.
14. C. S. Lewis, *Mere Christianity* (Fontana, 1952), p. 136.
15. John Brockington, *Hinduism and Christianity* (Macmillan,
    London, 1992), p. 175.
16. Letter to the Colossians 2:13–15.
17. Duryodhanana in *Pandavagita*, quoted by Acharya
    Dayaprakash, *Fulfilment of the Vedic Quest* (Lucknow, 1982),
    p. 29.
18. Letter to the Romans 8:20–2.
19. Paul's letter to the Ephesians 2:4–5.
20. Letter to the Hebrews 10:3,12.
21. Letter to the Romans 12:1; letter to the Hebrews 13:15.
22. Letter to the Hebrews 1:3.
23. Gospel of Matthew 18:20.
24. Y. D. Tiwari, in *Religion and Society*, September 1953,

pp. 113–20.
25. ibid.
26. Gospel of Mark 12:30, 31; Gospel of John 13:34.
27. *Gitanjali* xxxv.
28. K. M. Sen, *Hinduism: The World's Oldest Faith* (Pelican Books, London, 1961), p. 107.
29. Gospel of John 14:6.

Books for Further Information

Basham, A. L., *The Sacred Cow: The Evolution of Classical Hinduism*, edited by and annotated by Kenneth G. Zysk (Rider, 1989).
a clear summary of the early stages of Hinduism by one of the leading scholars of Indian culture.

Boyd, Robin, *An Introduction to Indian Christian Theology* (ISPCK, Delhi, 1969).
how Indian Christian thinkers have tried to relate the Bible and Christian thought to their Hindu background.

Burnett, David, *The Spirit of Hinduism* (Monarch Publications, Tunbridge Wells, 1992).
Cross, S., *The Elements of Hinduism* (Element, Dorset, 1994).
two clear introductory surveys. Burnett gives a historical perspective, while Cross has helpful material on philosophy, with particular emphasis on *Advaita Vedanta*.

Fuller, C. J., *The Camphor Flame: Popular Hinduism and Society in India* (Princeton University Press, Princeton, 1992).
the practice and meaning of popular Hindu worship, based on field research.

Gidoomal, Ram and Fearon, Mike, *Karma n' Chips* (Wimbledon Publishing Co., London, 1994).
a bold attempt to look at key Hindu concepts in the light of Christian faith, showing surprising similarities and contrasts.

Guptara, Prabhu and Osmaston, Amiel, *Yoga – A Christian Option?* (Grove Books Ltd, Nottingham, 1987).
a short dialogue on what *yoga* actually means and how it can be used, if at all.

Hopkins, T. J., *The Hindu Religious Tradition* (Wadsworth Publishing Co., Belmont, CA, 1971).
detailed and accurate study of the development of the different strands of Hindu thought and practice.

Jackson, Robert and Killingley, Dermont, *Approaches to Hinduism* (John Murray Publishers, 1988).
detailed survey of Hindu thought and practice today, with excellent lists of resources and suggestions for teaching.

Kanitkar, V. P. and Cole, Owen, *Hinduism* (Teach Yourself Books, Hodder and Stoughton, 1995).
clear and comprehensive, full of interesting detail and personal accounts by Hindus.

Mangalwadi, Vishal, *The World of Gurus* (revised edition Cornerstone Press, Chicago, 1992).
a study of key gurus, based on personal visits and research. The only survey of its kind.

Sarma, D. S., *Hinduism Through the Ages* (Bhavan Vidya Bhavan, Bombay, 1989).
survey of the Renaissance leaders of Hinduism, with a useful summary of the earlier periods as well.

Thomas, M. M., *The Acknowledged Christ of the Indian Renaissance* (The Christian Literature Society, Madras, 1970).
a fascinating study of the attitudes of Hindu Renaissance leaders to the person of Christ.

Zaehner, R. C., *Hinduism* (Oxford University Press, London, 1962).
an introduction to Hinduism, with excellent studies of the key words by a well-known scholar.

Glossary of Sanskrit Words

advaita – the school of Indian philosophy based upon non-duality and associated with the philosopher Sankara

Advaita Vedanta – the main philosophical school with Hinduism

ahimsa – non-violence

Alvar – poet saints of South India, linked with the later *Bhakti* movements

ananda – pure bliss, joy

artha – economic activity and profit – one of the goals in life

arti – worship involving the waving of lights before an image or images

asana – postures and exercises in *yoga*

ashram – a place of spiritual retreat and meditation, usually a community gathered around a holy person

ashrama – a stage in life, e.g. student stage, householder stage, etc.

atman – the inner Self in any creature, sometimes called the soul

avatar – a descent or incarnation of a god into a human or some other physical body

Bhagavad Gita – 'The Song of the Lord', the teachings given by Krishna to Arjuna. One of the most important texts in Hinduism.

Bhagwan – a name for the supreme God

bhajan – a worship song

bhakti – devotion to a god. *Bhakti marg* is one of the major paths to salvation

Brahma – the creator aspect of Brahman in the Hindu Trimurti (along with Vishnu and Shiva)

brahmacharya – the student stage of life of a twice-born Hindu

Brahman – the Ultimate Reality or Supreme God

Brahmanas – religious texts composed for the guidance of priests in the performance of Vedic sacrifices

Brahmin – a member of the highest social caste (*varna*); sometimes written as 'brahman'

chakra – the centres of psychic energy within a person, used in *tantra*

Christbhakti – worship of Christ

chit – consciousness

Dalit – 'opposed or broken', the name adopted by people formerly outside the caste system as a symbol of unity and solidarity

darshan – the meritorious viewing of a holy image or a person, gaining insight and blessing

devata – a minor deity

Devi – the Goddess, the feminine principle

dharma – righteousness, duty, the principle behind the universe, the basis of a person's religious and moral duty, according to their situation

Durga – the female goddess Devi in her fierce aspect

dvaita – the school of Hindu philosophy based upon the theistic teaching of duality

Ganesha – the elephant-headed son of Shiva and Parvati; god of prosperity and wisdom

Gayatri mantra – a hymn from the *Rig Veda*

Gita – religious song, often used as abbreviation for *Bhagavad Gita*

gryhasta – the second stage of life of a twice-born Hindu – the householder

guna – 'quality'; the three *gunas* are the fundamental qualities out of which all that exists is made

guru – teacher, spiritual guide

Harijan – 'people of God', the name given by Mahatma Gandhi for the 'Untouchables', the people outside the caste system

havan – a fire sacrifice where offerings are made

Indra – the Vedic god of war

ishtadevata – chosen deity, the god whom a person decides to worship in a special way

Isvara – 'the Lord', Brahman, known with qualities and worshipped

izzat – respect, honour

Jain – a member of the Jain religion

jati – hereditary groups within the caste system, usually people of the same occupation, marrying and dining together within their group

jiva – the individual soul

jivanmukta – one who is 'liberated in life', i.e. one who has realised his or her true nature as the *atman*

jnana – knowledge of God, spiritual knowledge; *jnana marg* is one of the major paths to salvation

kama – fulfilment of bodily desires, one of the goals in life

karma – 'action', the results of past action, the law of cause and effect in the moral realm

karma marg – one of the major paths to salvation

kirtan – gathering to sing worship songs

Krishna – the most popular *avatar* of Vishnu and hero of the *Mahabharata* (literally, 'black')

kshatriya – a member of the second group in the caste division

kundalini – in *tantra*, the life-energy symbolised as a serpent which needs to be awakened

lingam – a symbolic representation of the male organ denoting creative power, the most usual symbol of Shiva

Madhava – a philosopher who argued for the *dvaita* system, over against Sankara and Ramanuja

Mahabharata – one of the two great Hindu epics

mahatma – 'great soul', a title of respect

mandir – temple

mantra – sacred formula or sound used in meditation, always Sanskrit

Manu – the first man and lawgiver

marg – a path; the different ways to salvation are spoken of as paths

Mataji – Mother, the Mother Goddess

maya – nature of everyday reality, often translated as 'illusion', can also mean wisdom or God's power in the world *moksha* – the liberation of the soul from the successive series of births and deaths, the highest goal of life

mukti – salvation, liberation (sometimes equivalent to *moksha*)

murti – an image or picture of a deity

Nirguna – unmanifest, without attributes, used of Brahman

nishkama karma – action without desire or attachment, an important concept in the *Bhagavad Gita*

OM – the sacred syllable – it is believed to contain the sound of all reality; used during meditation

paramatman – the supreme spirit

Prajapati – the creator of the universe and lord of the creatures

prakriti – the original substance of the universe from which all matter comes

pranayama – control of breathing in yoga

prasad – blessed food distributed among the worshippers at the end of *puja*

puja – a common form of Hindu worship

punya – merit

Puranas – ancient texts containing many Hindu myths and stories about Hindu gods

purusa – the primeval man

rajas – one of the three *gunas* or qualities

Rama – son of King Dasaratha, regarded as an incarnation of Vishnu, also called Ram

Ramanuja – a philosopher who argued for the system of *vishishtadvaita*

Ramayana – one of the two great Hindu epics telling the story of Rama

Rig Veda – the first and most ancient of the Vedic texts

rta – the divine order which integrates the cosmos

roop – form, aspect, the way in which God or gods manifest themselves

sadhu – a general term for a holy man or ascetic

Saguna – manifest God, with attributes, used of Brahman

samadhi – a trance; a state of pure consciousness of oneness with God

sanatana – eternal

Sanatana Dharma – the ancient and eternal way of life

sanatana sat guru – the Eternal and Living Way (Jesus Christ)

Sankara – a philosopher who argued for the system of *advaita*

Sankhya – a school of Hindu philosophy which divides the universe into inert *purusa* and active *prakriti*

sannyas – the fourth stage in a Hindu man's life; see *sannyasi*

sannyasi – a person who gives up his name, family ties, and possessions, and devotes his life to meditation in order to attain *moksha*

sansara – the cycle of successive births, deaths, and rebirths

sarvodaya – 'benefit of all', a concept emphasised by Mahatma Gandhi

sat – truth, reality

sati – (literally, 'true ones'), used for Hindu wives who immolated themselves on their husbands' funeral pyres

satsang – 'truth together', a gathering to sing or discuss spiritual matters

sattva – one of the three *gunas* or qualities

satya – truth

satyagraha – 'truth-force', a method of passive resistance or civil disobedience used by Mahatma Gandhi

Shaivism – the worship of the god Shiva

shakti – energy or the feminine principle

shanti – peace

Shiva – one of the two great gods of Hinduism, along with Vishnu (and Brahma)

sloka – a verse or short section of scripture

smriti – 'that which is remembered', the other scriptures apart from the *Vedas*

soma – the juice of a plant with special powers, mentioned in the *Rig Veda*

sruti – 'that which is heard', i.e. the *Vedas*

sudra – the fourth group in the caste system

swami – honorific title before the name of a teacher or holy person

Swaminarayan – literally meaning 'Lord God', the name of a Hindu movement followed by a significant number of Gujerati Hindus

swarga – a name for heaven, where some people who have gained merit go temporarily

tamas – one of the three *gunas*

tantra – the texts forming the basis for the tantric tradition, or that tradition itself. *Tantra* emphasises *shakti*, the feminine principle

tapas – power, or heat generated by yogic meditation

trimurti – the three forms or aspects of supreme reality in relation to the world; the gods Brahma, the Creator, Vishnu, the Preserver, and Shiva, the Destroyer

tulsi – a plant with medicinal qualities, considered to be sacred and grown in most Hindu homes

Tulsidas – poet who composed a version of *Ramayana*

Upanishad – a set of holy texts of philosophy and religion, the end of the *Vedas*

Vaishnavism – the worship of the god Vishnu

vaisya – the third group in the caste system

vanaprastha – the third stage of life, retirement and focus on spiritual matters

varna – 'colour', the name used for the caste system with four major divisions

Varnashrama dharma – the way of life based on caste and stages of life

Vedanta – (literally 'The end of the *Vedas*'), the final philosophy of the *Vedas* as expressed in the *Upanishads*

Vedas – the Hindu scriptures consisting of the *Rig Veda*, the *Yajar Veda*, the *Sama Veda*, the *Atharva Veda*; also the *Brahmanas* and the *Upanishads*

vishishtadvaita – modified non-duality or modified monism, a system associated with Ramanuja which modified the strict *advaita* of Sankara

Vishnu – one of the two great gods of Hinduism, along with Shiva (and Brahma)

vishva – 'universal', used in the title of the organisation *Vishwa Hindu Parishad*, meaning universal Hindu organisation

yoga – 'union', a system of philosophy combining physical exercises and meditation

yoni – symbolic representation of the female organ, usually

with the *lingam*
yuga – an age of the world; there are four *yugas*, each worse
than the last

Index

Bold figures indicate the more significant references.